Architecture and Polyphony:
Building in the Islamic World Toda

Thames & Hudson

The Aga Khan Award for Architecture

Contents

Acknowledgements

This monograph was coordinated by Prince Hussain
Aga Khan, Farrokh Derakhshani and Jack Kennedy on
behalf of the Steering Committee of the 2004 Aga Khan
Award for Architecture.

All texts were edited by Philippa Baker. Project texts
are based on reports prepared by the 2004 Award
On-Site Project Reviewers and edited by Philippa
Baker with assistance from Christine Davis, Sarah
Polden and Kirsty Seymour-Ure.

Design and layout of the book were undertaken by
Irma Boom with Sonja Haller.

First published in the United Kingdom in 2004 by
Thames & Hudson Ltd, 181A High Holborn,
London WC1V 7QX
www.thamesandhudson.com

© 2004 Thames & Hudson Ltd, London, and
The Aga Khan Award for Architecture, Geneva.

British Library Cataloguing-in-Publication Data.
A catalogue record for this book is available from
the British Library.

ISBN 0-500-28533-0

Designed by Irma Boom Office, Amsterdam
Printed and bound in Singapore by CS Graphics

Inside cover: Collages from the Jury Meetings
by Ghada Amer

The 2004 Aga Khan Award for Architecture

The year 2004 marks the completion of the ninth triennial cycle of the Aga Khan Award for Architecture, established in 1977 by His Highness the Aga Khan. During the twenty-seven years since it was founded, the Award has responded to the constant changes that have taken place in Muslim societies throughout the world. The results of this cycle of the Award reveal a renewed sense of confidence and hope in the contributions that Muslims today make to architecture and society throughout the world, even while retaining their cultural specificity and identity.

The Award Steering Committee

This cycle of the Award has been characterized by a commitment to pluralism and tolerance, with a focus on recognizing architectural achievements that demonstrate the highest international standards of excellence in building. The Award Steering Committee, chaired by the Aga Khan, worked intensely throughout the current cycle, beginning with a review and revision of the eligibility requirements projects should meet in order to be considered. These requirements were then communicated to over a thousand nominators who recommend projects to the Award office. They include an emphasis on innovative types of architecture emerging throughout the Muslim world – projects that may be large-scale or modest in scope and that demonstrate new directions for architecture, planning and landscaping in both urban and rural contexts. The Steering Committee acknowledged that such projects do not fit easily into any single category, but embrace a variety of programmes and building types. The Committee also placed importance on projects by young architects and on the categories of infrastructure, landscaping, community development and public urban spaces. In particular, the Committee asked nominators to give special attention to projects that respond to the growing housing crisis in many Muslim societies. New types of project – productive territories, active landscapes or land-reclamation projects – were also recommended, and the Steering Committee expressed specific interest in locality and contemporary conditions.

To be eligible for the Ninth Award Cycle, projects must have been completed during the twelve-year period from 1991 to 2002 and in use for at least one full year between the period 1 January 1991 and 31 December 2002. No projects may be considered that are commissioned by His Highness the Aga Khan or undertaken by current members of the Award Steering Committee, Master Jury or Award staff, or by the Board or staff of the Aga Khan Trust for Culture.

The nomination process yielded a total of 378 eligible projects, located in forty-four countries, and these formed the basis of the first week-long meeting of the 2004 Master Jury during January 2004. The Master Jury – an independent and autonomous group appointed by the Steering Committee – comprised nine men and women from throughout the world, including practising architects, structural engineers, artists, historians, philosophers and experts in urban planning and restoration.

Issues and criteria

In order to explain the objectives and procedures of the Award, the Steering Committee met with the members of the Jury before the latter's review of projects and subsequent deliberations. In a written note to the Jury Members, the Steering Committee indicated its belief that all of the finalist projects should meet a number of 'threshold criteria', <u>contributing to established ways of doing things or extending boundaries in the field, making intelligent use of available resources and materials and responding sensitively to the environment, and showing social and ethical responsibility with respect to individual and community self-determination.</u>

The Steering Committee also identified a number of issues that emerged in the course of discussions during the Ninth Award Cycle as important factors in current architectural practice in the Islamic world. These were: <u>the symbolization of power and authority (dealing with issues of power relations); the articulation of public and private spaces; issues of cultural identity and cultural representation; sensitivity to plurality; and constructive aspirations for individuals and societies.</u>

The issues put forward by the Steering Committee were intended to stimulate initial conversation among the Jury Members. Reconfirming the Master Jury's independent and autonomous mandate, the Committee noted that it was the Jury Members' responsibility to determine which, if any, of the criteria and suggested issues were pertinent to their deliberations. The Steering Committee noted that it would be unlikely for any individual project to meet all of the threshold criteria and deal with all of the issues proposed, but expressed hope that the projects selected for Awards by the Master Jury would be recognizable by their thoughtful approach to one or more of the criteria.

To avoid inadvertently affecting the Jury's decision-making process by the imposition of classifications such as building type or location, the Steering Committee requested that the 378 nominated projects be presented in alphabetical order by name of architect or architectural firm.

The 2004 Award Master Jury

As a result of their first meeting, the nine Master Jury members selected twenty-three projects for further study as part of the Award's On-Site Project Review Programme. All of the twenty-three shortlisted projects were visited on site between February and May 2004 by experts appointed by the Award. These Project Reviewers prepared written reports and at the second Master Jury meeting, in June 2004, made half-hour presentations on each project and discussed particular points of interest raised by the Jury. Deliberations continued in private sessions over the following four days and resulted in the Jury's selection of seven projects to share the 2004 Aga Khan Award for Architecture. The Jury's decisions were unanimous.

Architecture and Polyphony: Building in the Islamic World Today

This book was designed by Irma Boom. All texts were edited by Philippa Baker with the assistance of Prince Hussain Aga Khan. Features on the seven winning projects include descriptions and illustrations of each project, with texts based on the reports by the On-Site Reviewers. The written Statement of the Award Master Jury is integral to understanding the collective significance of the seven projects, and an Introduction to the Statement by the Chair of the Jury, Professor Farshid Moussavi, describes the nature and challenges of the Jury discussions and deliberations in a more personal fashion. Many of the Jury Members have contributed essays to this volume, developing their professional or personal views about architecture and its condition in Muslim societies today. Reflecting the breadth and diversity of the Award process, the two philosophers on the Jury – professors Modjtaba Sadria and Reinhard Schulze – have contributed writings that situate the role of architecture in the wider realm of contemporary society. Artist Ghada Amer, also a member of the Jury, has prepared a visual interpretation of the eleven days of Jury meetings during January and June 2004. The volume concludes with an essay, 'Architecture without Building', by Steering Committee member Babar Khan Mumtaz, while 'A Breakthrough', by Dr Suha Özkan, Secretary General of the Award, situates the current winning projects within the larger perspective of the nine completed Award cycles.

The Aga Khan Development Network

His Highness the Aga Khan, forty-ninth hereditary Imam of the Shia Ismaili Muslims, is the Chairman of the Aga Khan Development Network, a group of agencies working in health, education, culture and rural and economic development, primarily in Asia and Africa. The Aga Khan Trust for Culture, of which the Aga Khan Award for Architecture is a part, undertakes the Network's cultural programmes.

Introduction to the Statement of the Award Master Jury
Farshid Moussavi, Chair of the Jury

It is an honour to represent the Master Jury and I thank the Steering Committee on behalf of the Jury for giving us this opportunity to reflect on and learn from architectural processes and interventions in the Muslim world and to contribute through the Award towards the enhancement of the environment. The composition of the Master Jury is a microcosm of conditions in Muslim societies as well as the world at large – a vortex of people, cultures, ages, expectations, architectural heritage, economics. Architecture, we believe, needs to develop a variety of tools to respond to this plural, multifaceted condition. The composition of the Jury was determined by the Steering Committee. The Jury therefore recognizes the conditions the Steering Committee has tried to create in bringing the Jury Members together. But of course this also means that the Steering Committee is responsible for the outcome!

Selecting the winning projects was an exhausting experience but also very interesting and we even managed to enjoy it. The two philosophers in the group were geographically placed in the room in such a way as to sandwich and shape the rest of us, who represent more intuitive, creative and artistic approaches. They were constantly trying to broaden the field in which architecture operates beyond the mere act of building and technical perfection to include issues such as politics, identity, cross-cultural exchange, pluralism and public investment. The designers, architects, engineers and artists on the Jury were superexcited by this power that the philosophers were bestowing on architecture. It felt as if architecture could still play a central role in our societies and that everything is possible – that our role need not be reduced to the mere act of building but might also include facilitating larger processes that are latent in this complex and rich context.

But we did not submit entirely to this broader view, knowing that one of the powerful ways in which architecture can improve the environment is in the way it transfers and crystallizes these processes into form. And at the same time, if we are committed to innovation, we must look at projects at every level of detail. <u>Innovation rarely happens in a vacuum; it happens only intermittently, in response to acute conditions and the consolidation of problems that arise out of various cultures</u>. So innovation may be necessary at the 'macro' scale or at the 'micro' scale of delivering an architectural solution.

We were also interested in recognizing architectural processes as well as architectural ideas that symbolize the Muslim world. After all, we all know that ideas make up only ten per cent of an architectural venture. Architects are more like sailors who are constantly against a sea of odds, such as project managers who want to 'value engineer' the scheme, budgets that are never big enough, politicians who are single-minded, public consultations that subject a scheme to selfish perspectives, time… So for us as a group, the architect's skill in guiding this process is as important as his or her original ideas.

One of the ways in which we think the Award should extend is to be not only the mechanism to acknowledge outstanding results but also an initiator – <u>a platform for seeds of ideas that show the potential to trigger improvement and enhancement of the environment in Muslim societies</u>.

Statement of the Award Master Jury

The Jury met for the first time in January 2004 and started by reviewing 378 projects that had been nominated for the Ninth Cycle of the Aga Khan Award for Architecture. After vigorous and concentrated discussions, the Jury shortlisted twenty-three projects that were proposed for On-Site Project Review. During the second meeting, in June 2004, the Reviewers presented to the Jury their detailed reports and, after discussions, the Jury selected seven projects to receive the 2004 Aga Khan Award for Architecture.

From the outset, the Jury agreed that they would need to seek out a comprehensive approach in order to discover, understand and explain the challenges of architecture in the Muslim world as it confronts modernity in all its diversity. Four areas of social meaning came to the fore, and the Jury expressed these as a series of questions.

The first question raises the issue of how the complexity of history and of historical memory can be expressed in architecture. Because restoration deals with history in architectural terms, it tends, pragmatically, not simply to freeze the past as it may have existed at a given moment. Instead, restoration increasingly responds to the needs of present-day groups and individuals, who often use historic buildings for new purposes. By accommodating historical meaning and contemporary needs, a building retains social meaning rather than becoming simply an object of tourism.

Secondly, the Jury considered the question of how private initiatives are integrated into the emerging public sphere. The Jury believes that the development of a pluralist public realm is one of the most important issues facing many Muslim countries. Today, more and more private initiatives in the public realm empower societies and address their needs, be it in the fields of education, sanitation or other social requirements. Architecture plays an important role in manifesting these endeavours, and the Jury particularly appreciated a balanced relationship between the social content of an initiative and its architectural representation.

The winning projects also address the question of how to express individuality in complex social settings. In modernity, architecture expresses individuality, permitting a poetical interpretation of the self. The Jury recognized the growing awareness and appreciation of individuality in the Muslim world. On the one hand, this individuality counters the idea that Muslim societies emphasize collective identities; on the other, it reveals the plurality of Muslim traditions.

The fourth question the Jury considered was the issue of how power and authority in the global domains of technology, culture and economics might be addressed through architecture. The Jury paid special attention to the responsibility of architecture in the Muslim world and to projects that show understanding of the worldwide exchange of technological, cultural and economic knowledge in local contexts. The translation of global identities into architecture – which can occur in the technology used in buildings or in the potential functions of buildings – was considered by the Jury to be of great importance for many parts of the Muslim world.

The Jury also analysed <u>how these four issues have been transferred to architecture</u>. It is common sense that the way structure and design are used in a project should always be adequate to the issue addressed. Adequacy, however, does not mean simply assigning a form to a problem and updating traditional architectural solutions. It means adopting a critical perspective on the problem and addressing it by means of architectural techniques. The Jury recognized this by giving importance to projects that raise the standards of excellence.

Finally, the Jury focused on the social, cultural and environmental impact of the projects, analysing the balance between intention and realization, meaning and material, and functionality and use. The integration of projects within the environment and the criticism of tradition were also factors in assessing projects.

<u>Architecture in the Muslim world partakes of all the features of modernity in architecture</u>. However, it often also tries to incorporate specific Islamic meanings, and it is only in such deliberate instances that architecture can be labelled 'Islamic'. When 'Islamic' traditions are followed instinctively, the result is simply architecture in a Muslim cultural context. This means that there is a difference between architecture in the Muslim world and what is defined in discourse as 'Islamic architecture'. The plurality of architecture in the Muslim world is evident at many levels: in varied discourses on architecture; in architecture that deals with restoration in ways that re-establish the generic pluralism of Muslim culture; and in the multiplicity of forms produced by a variety of social, cultural and economic environments. <u>The Jury was particularly aware of the complexity of the plurality of the Muslim world and was critical of those projects that tried to establish a cultural normativity that could threaten that plurality</u>.

The Jury believes that all seven projects selected for the 2004 Aga Khan Award for Architecture meet with the foregoing criteria.

Ghada Amer
Hanif Kara
Rahul Mehrotra
Farshid Moussavi
Modjtaba Sadria
Reinhard Schulze
Elías Torres Tur
Billie Tsien
Jafar Tukan

Geneva, June 2004

84–101
Old City of Jerusalem
Revitalization Programme
Jerusalem

102–119
B2 House
Ayvacik, Turkey

32–49
Gando Primary School
Gando, Burkina Faso

66–83
Restoration of
Al-Abbas Mosque
Asnaf, Yemen

14–31
Bibliotheca Alexandrina
Alexandria, Egypt

Recipients of the 2004 Aga Khan Award for Architecture

120–137
Petronas Towers
Kuala Lumpur, Malaysia
50–65
Sandbag Shelter Prototypes
Various locations

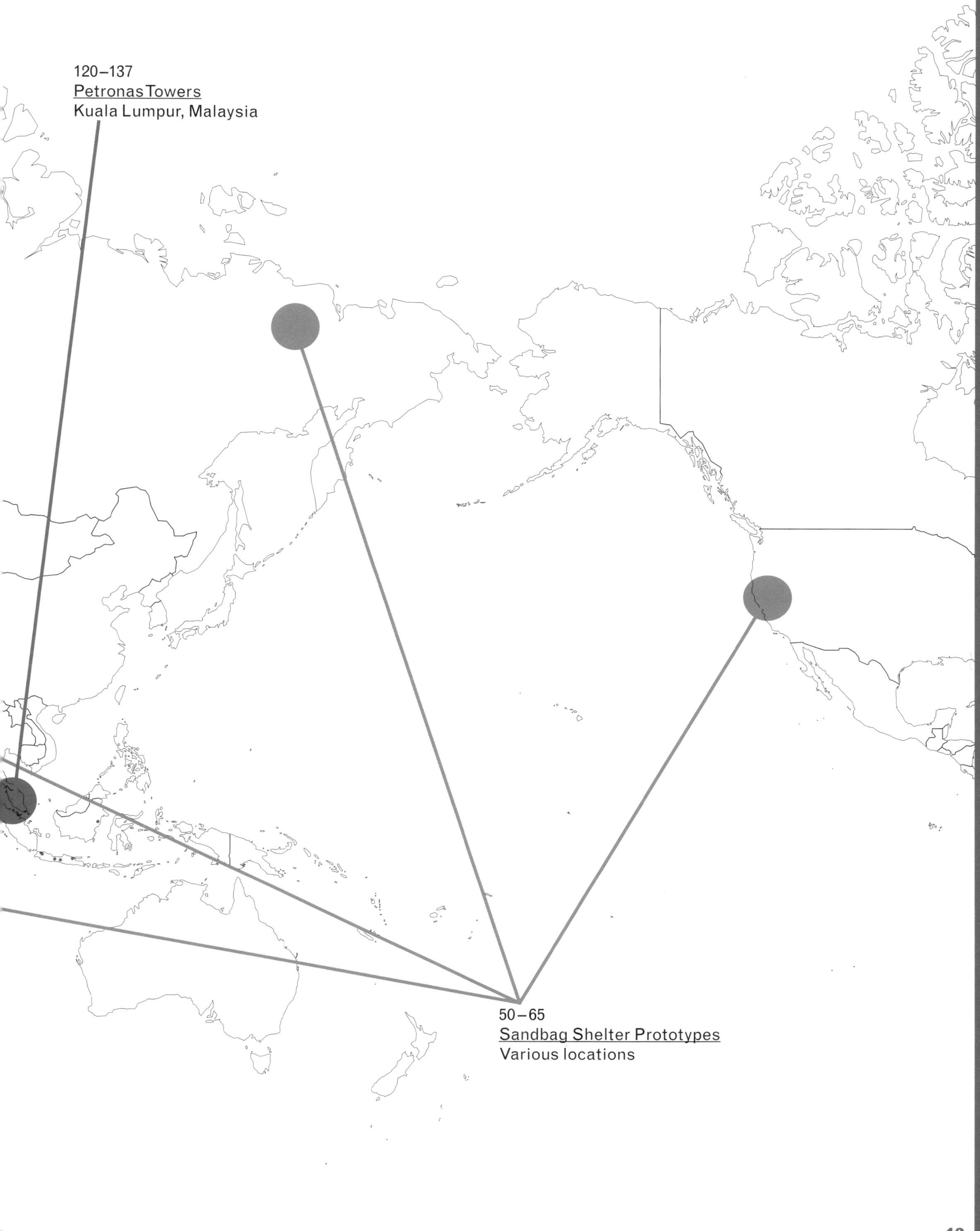

Alexandria, Egypt

Bibliotheca Alexandrina

The Bibliotheca Alexandrina is a revival of the legendary ancient library built in classical Greek times. The rebuilding of the library has returned Alexandria to its former status as a centre for learning and exchange and provided the city with a landmark building. The new library also serves as the world's window on Egypt, Egypt's window on the world and a library for the new digital age.

The symbolism of the library's simple tilted disc form has a strong and universally recognizable resonance, as well as allowing for the creation of an impressive space without overpowering the visitor or the city behind it. Internally the library is large in size but always human in scale, clear in organization but flexible in use, grand in conception but beautifully detailed.

The spirit of international cooperation in which the library was conceived, funded, designed and implemented has been maintained in its management to create an institution that is truly global in its outlook. At the same time, the building is technically outstanding – its substructure comprising the largest circular diaphragm wall in the world. The rich programmes that it houses, from specialist libraries to museums and various focused research centres, promise to make it a centre of scholarship for the region.

Bibliotheca Alexandrina

This building has received an Award because it shows an innovative approach to the design and placement of a large, symbolic form on one of the most important waterfronts in the world. From its inception through an international competition to its design and construction by many international companies, and in its current financial management, the project provides a model for other such projects in bringing together the international community and encouraging cooperation and commitment from society as a whole.

While the building is groundbreaking in architectural and technological terms, it also responds sensitively to a wide spectrum of issues, including politics, religion, culture and history. The bold 'tilted disc' forms an icon while delivering a highly formal and monumental building. The technical challenges of constructing such a large development close to the water's edge and within an urban setting have been embraced and dealt with through the use of advanced technologies. The form also provides a clear organization and functions well for the rich variety of programmes it houses, while acting as a catalyst for improvements throughout the city. Finally, the project celebrates learning and brings knowledge to societies across all cultures, playing a crucial role in the progress of civilization.

The ancient library of Alexandria was once the most famous library in the world. Built by Ptolemy I Soter ('Saviour') (ca 366–ca 283 BC), a Macedonian general in the army of Alexander the Great, it was the first universal library and at its peak is said to have held 700,000 scrolls in various languages. It was here that the Old Testament was first translated into Greek and that Euclid wrote his *Elements*.

Today Alexandria, stretching 70 kilometres along the Mediterranean coast, is Egypt's main port, forming a large industrial and commercial centre and an important summer resort. In 1974, the University of Alexandria began a campaign for the rebuilding of the ancient library, choosing the current site, which is believed to be close to the original location. Egypt's President Mubarak took up the project at a national level in 1988, and an international competition, organized by the Egyptian government and the International Union of Architects, was won by the Norwegian company Snøhetta in 1989. Detailed archaeological excavations of the site were carried out before construction began in 1995, and the building opened in October 2002.

In rebuilding the library, the main aim was to return Alexandria to the glory it had enjoyed in ancient times, creating an institution that would become famous throughout the region for the quality of its services and the wealth of its resources. The scheme was required to provide a main reading room for 2,000 readers, six specialist libraries, three museums, seven research centres, three permanent galleries, space for temporary exhibitions, a planetarium, a public plaza, offices, a cafeteria and all the necessary facilities and services required for such a complex.

The project is located in the ancient royal quarter of the original Greek city, now part of the town centre. To the north is the coast road and to the south a street where some of the university's faculty buildings are located, with further buildings to the east and west. It was important that the building should respond to the scale of the surrounding fabric and, to this end, the library was designed as a tilting disc rising from the ground, with four levels below ground and seven above. The scale of the building is thus minimized at close quarters, so it does not overwhelm the visitor.

The form also has strong symbolic significance: the circle is found in all cultures, relating to the heavenly bodies through which humans first understood the passage of time in relation to the movement of the sun, moon and stars. As it passes into the ground, the building suggests the past and, as it rises from the earth, it looks towards the future, while the ground itself represents the present. The tilted disc also creates an iconic presence on the otherwise homogenous skyline of the coastal road and the structure is easily visible from across the bay. Its exterior wall is clad with four thousand granite blocks carved with letters from the alphabets of the world. The panels were quarried by splitting the rock to create a wavy texture and the designs were traced by computer but carved by hand.

The project comprises two main parts: the library and the planetarium. These are linked at basement level, beneath a public plaza, to an existing conference centre, while a pedestrian bridge spans the plaza between the university and the coastal road. The library building is clearly organized, with the eastern sector of the disc housing the main reading area, and the western segment comprising the entrance, administrative area, specialized libraries and museums, as well as other facilities and services. A segment cut out of one edge of the circle, facing the plaza, is glazed to allow light into the building.

The main reading area is a single open space with eight terraces, each accommodating a different subject section, starting from the roots of knowledge (philosophy, history, religion, geography) and ending with the latest technologies. Because the new structure crosses so many ages and cultures, the architects aimed to make its form universal. However, in reference to Egypt's Islamic heritage, they also sought to create a space that, like religious Islamic architecture, is conducive to meditative thinking while accommodating large groups of people. The terraces break down the scale of the reading area for the individuals working in their own spaces, but also overlook the whole expanse of the room.

The project acknowledges the presence of the sea by setting the public square along the coastal road. The planetarium, with seating for ninety-nine people, consists of a suspended sphere that forms the main focus of the plaza. The plaza is also planted with twelve olive trees, symbolizing peace, while a pool surrounding the library on three sides connects ground and sky in its reflection and serves to further delineate the building's form

The substructure of the library is the most innovative part of the project. The half submersion of the building 18 metres below ground on a site close to the sea raised serious structural problems. It circular diaphragm wall is considered the largest in the world, with a diameter of 160 metres and a height of 35 metres. The varying temperature differentials along the wall's length presented further complications, and the design was analyzed using computer modelling to resolve this issue. The wall has horizontal reinforcements but no expansion joints, minimizing the risk of water penetration. The uplift forces from the groundwater and the eccentric loading on the foundations – the north side of the library bears only one floor whereas the south side carries the load of all eleven floors and the books – meant that the risk of the building tilting was great. Hence the foundations are unique in that they were designed as tension piles with a heavy raft foundation on the south side and as compression piles to take the weight on the north side. The superstructure, however, is a fairly standard system of a concrete frame and infill panels, with columns cast in situ and pre-cast capitals and beams. The structures of the planetarium and bridge are of steel.

Computer technology was used in designing a number of elements of the building, including its form, which is toroidal rather than cylindrical. One of the most successful features of the building is its use of natural light, drawn in through glazed roof panels. The orientation of the roof panels was carefully studied on computer at the design stage to introduce maximum levels of natural light without direct sunlight. Glare is reduced through glass shades over the windows.

Another key innovation in the project is the universality of its conception. An international competition was organized to secure the best design. In 1990, the Declaration of Aswan called for international support for the project and it was funded by donations from the Arab world and twenty-seven other countries. After an initial design phase, architects Snøhetta formed a consortium with the Egyptian engineering specialists Hamza Associates, with whom they developed the project and supervised the work. Throughout construction, foreign and local consultants worked closely together, a commitment that is reflected in the quality of detailing in the building and that has raised standards in Egypt's construction industry. Finally, the library is organized as an independent entity, with a council of patrons headed by the president of Egypt and including various heads of state and eminent international figures. Under this arrangement, the library is financially independent and has a high international profile.

The library has also prompted improvements throughout the city, such as renovating roads, building bridges and upgrading hotels. The legal infrastructure and high profile of the project, its emphasis on employing and training young people, and its sound financial footing all ensure the future standing of the Bibliotheca Alexandrina and hence its long-term influence and impact on the social and cultural life of the city.

Most of the library's users are students from the University of Alexandria and local schools. They are proud of their library, seeing it as a modern, up-to-the-minute project that connects them to the contemporary world. The building is admired for its simplicity and strength of form, for its main reading area, for the quality of light and high standard of construction, and for the coordination of the complex work and the high standards of detailing. Various conferences held in the complex have received regional and international attention, raising the profile of the whole city. The library is seen as a progressive landmark for the country as a whole, reinstating Egypt's position as an open, modern centre of cultural exchange.

Bibliotheca Alexandrina
Port Said Street, El-Shatby,
Alexandria, Egypt

Client
Bibliotheca Alexandrina, Egypt (H.E. President
Hosni Mubarak, Chair, Council of Patrons; H.E.
Mrs Suzanne Mubarak, Chair, Board of Trustees;
Ismaïl Serageldin, Director; Mohsen Zahran,
Project Director, General Organization for
the Alexandria Library, 1995–2001).

Sponsors
Government of Egypt; Ministry of Education,
Egypt; University of Alexandria, Egypt;
United Nations Educational, Scientific,
and Cultural Organization, France.

Architects
Snøhetta Hamza Consortium, Egypt: Craig
Dykers, Christoph Kapeller and Kjetil Trædal
Thorsen, Principal Architects, Snøhetta
AS, Norway; Mohamed Sharkass, Head of
Architecture, Hamza Associates, Egypt.

Engineers
Hamza Associates, Egypt: Mamdouh Hamza,
Chairman and geotechnical engineer;
Mashhour Ghunaim and Ahmed Rashed,
structural engineers; Ibrahim Helal, electrical
engineer; Ali Omar, mechanical engineer;
Mohsen Abdou, plumbing and fire-fighting
engineer; Tarek Yassine, site engineer.

Consultants
Jorunn Sannes, Norway, fine arts for stone wall;
Schumann Smith, UK, management cost and
specifications; Lichtdesign, Germany, custom
lighting design; Multiconsult, Norway, acoustics;
Warrington Fire Research, UK, fire and life safety;
Stewart Helms, UK, security.

Contractors
Radio Trevi, Italy; Arab Contractors, Egypt;
Balfour Beatty, UK.

Competition	September 1989
Commission	February 1994
Design	May 1994–February 1996
Construction	May 1995–July 2001
Official inauguration	October 2002

Site Area	45,000m²
Built area	85,405m²

Cost	US$218,000,000

Snøhetta Hamza Consortium is a joint venture
of Snøhetta AS, a Norwegian firm, and Hamza
Associates, an Egyptian firm, specially established for the Bibliotheca Alexandrina. Snøhetta
AS, is an architectural, landscaping and interior
architecture agency, founded in 1989. Snøhetta
co-founders Craig Dykers (b. 1961, Germany),
Christoph Kapeller (b. 1956, Austria) and
Kjetil Trædal Thorsen (b. 1958, Norway) won
the international competition for the Library of
Alexandria in 1989 and saw the project through
to completion. Since then, they have realized
a number of major public buildings in Norway
and throughout the world, including the
Lillehammer Olympic Museum (1993), Karmøy
Fishing Museum (1998) and Sandvika Culture
Centre (2003), all in Norway, and the Institute
for Neurobiology for the Mediterranean (INMED)
in Marseilles (2003). Hamza Associates is one of
Egypt's leading consultancies, a multi-disciplinary
engineering firm established in 1979 by Mamdouh
Hamza, with over 460 major projects in Egypt,
Africa and the Middle East, including ports
and marine facilities, energy and power plants,
irrigation and hydraulic structures, transportation facilities, public buildings, tourist and
sports facilities, urban, regional and rural
planning projects, water-supply and sanitation
facilities, and numerous rehabilitation,
upgrading and environmental schemes.

Websites
Bibliotheca Alexandrina
www.bibalex.org
Snøhetta AS
www.snoarc.no
Hamza Associates
www.hamza.org

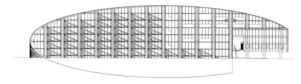

elevation

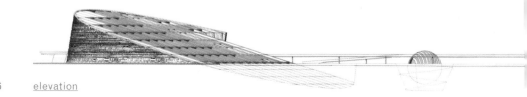

elevation

section

section

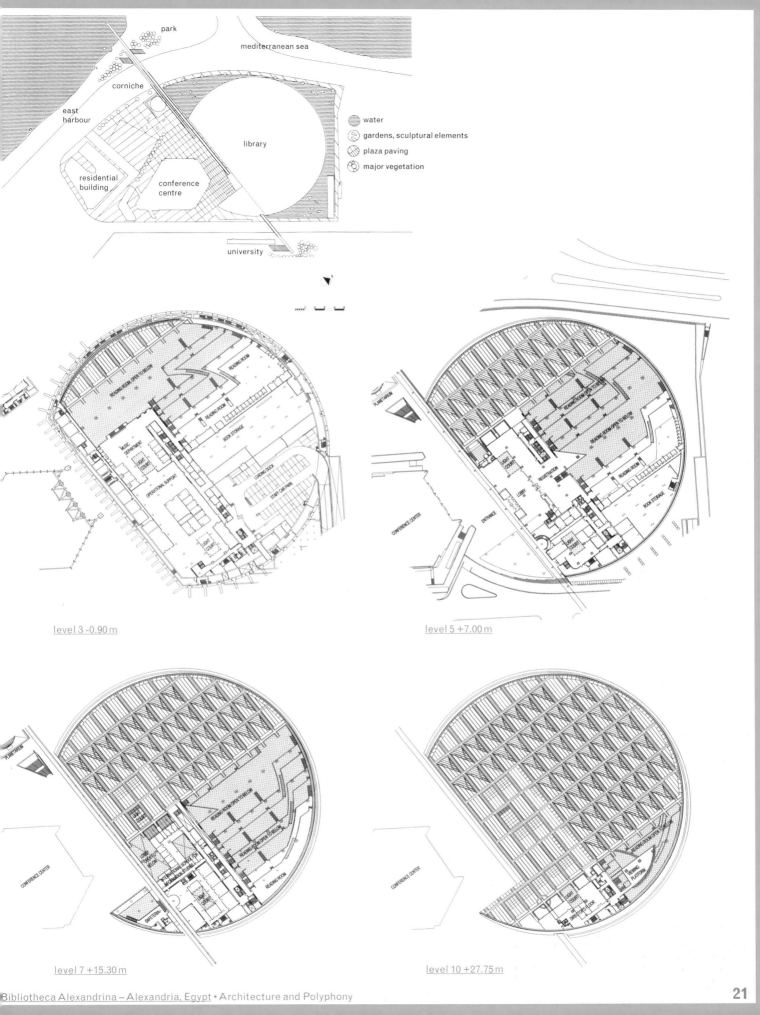

park

mediterranean sea

corniche

east
harbour

library

○ water

○ gardens, sculptural elements

○ plaza paving

○ major vegetation

residential
building

conference
centre

university

level 3 -0.90 m

level 5 +7.00 m

level 7 +15.30 m

level 10 +27.75 m

Gando, Burkina Faso

Gando Primary School

This school in the south of Burkina Faso is the result of one man's mission to improve conditions in his village. Not only did he design the school and raise the funds to build it; he also secured government support to train people in building with local materials, and drew on a strong tradition of community solidarity to engage all of the villagers in the construction of this school for their children. The school successfully combines the modern architectural language learned by the architect in his studies abroad with traditional techniques and materials to create a building that is both elegant and appropriate to its context. The main building material is local earth blocks, while a light metal roof structure was devised that was easy to execute, requiring only simple tools. Comfort is ensured by low-cost passive cooling techniques – cross-ventilation, orientation and an overhanging roof. The community has been empowered by its involvement with the project, learning skills that can now be applied elsewhere as well as gaining a school that has attracted children from outside the village and provided an example for other such projects in the surrounding area.

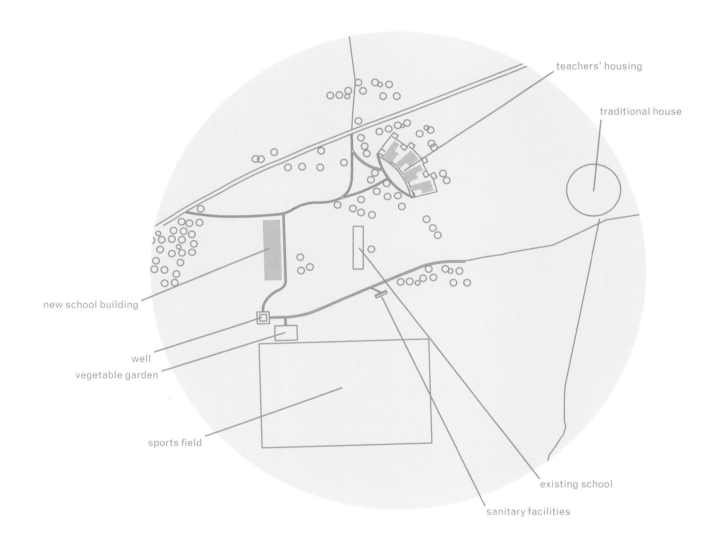

teachers' housing

traditional house

new school building

well

vegetable garden

sports field

existing school

sanitary facilities

This project has received an Award for its elegant architectonic clarity, achieved with the most humble of means and materials, and for its transformative value. Located in a remote settlement of Burkina Faso, the school is the result of a vision that was first articulated by the architect and then embraced by his community. The first person from his village with access to higher education, while studying architecture in Berlin the architect became determined to design and build the school. Securing funding for materials from supporters in Germany, he mobilized the men, women and children of the village to erect the building. The result is a structure of grace, warmth and sophistication, in sympathy with the local climate and culture. The practical and the poetic are fused. The primary school in Gando inspires pride and instils hope in its community, laying the foundations for the advancement of a people.

Gando, with a population of 3,000, lies on the southern plains of Burkina Faso, some 200 kilometres from Ouagadougou, the capital. Set in an expanse of scrubby savannah with patches of agricultural land, it is a typical village of the region, comprising about forty round compounds that contain numerous one-room structures, built of sun-dried mud blocks – *banco* – and arranged around a central area. The compound structures are typically covered with flat mud roofs or pitched tin roofs, while some are thatched, as is the case with the granaries, which are always raised above ground to escape damp and pests. The main entrances to the compounds are marked by arbours – *zandi* – or large trees, known as 'palaver trees', where the men of the village gather to talk.

In 1990, as part of governmental development measures, Gando was provided with a primary school – a modest building of concrete blocks roofed with corrugated metal sheeting. In spite of the program-matic success of the initiative, the building's low quality, combined with lack of government funding for its maintenance, soon brought it to an advanced state of disrepair, threatening its survival.

Diébédo Francis Kéré was the first person from Gando to study abroad. He was convinced that education was the cornerstone of his people's advancement. As an architecture student in Berlin, he took upon himself the cause of ensuring that his village would not be deprived of a school, determining that a new school should be designed in sympathy with the local climate, resources and materials.

Local financing was out of the question: neither the community as a whole nor any of its residents had the necessary means. Therefore, while in Germany, Kéré and a group of friends set up a fund-raising association, Schulbausteine für Gando (Bricks for the Gando School). The idea of building a school in the middle of Africa met with a positive response. Having secured finance through the association, Kéré obtained, in Burkina Faso, the support of LOCOMAT, a government agency engaged in the promotion of local building materials, to train brick-makers in the technique of working with compressed stabilized earth. Construction began in October 2000, carried out largely by the village's men, women and children. After the school was completed in July 2001, construction of buildings for resident teachers began along similar principles.

In order to achieve sustainability, the project was based on the principles of designing for climatic comfort with low-cost construction, making the most of local materials and the potential of the local community, and adapting technology from the industrialized world in a simple way. Underlying the project was a strong didactic component: it was designed as an exemplar that would raise awareness in the local community of the merits of traditional materials, updated with simple techniques that would need few new skills.

The school building includes three volumes, each containing a class-room measuring 7 x 9 metres. The classrooms are arranged in a linear fashion and separated by covered outdoor areas that can be used for teaching and play. The structure comprises traditional load-bearing walls made from stabilized and compressed earth blocks. Concrete beams run across the width of the structure, and steel bars lying across these support a ceiling also of compressed earth blocks. The whole is protected by a single roof, comprising a space frame of steel trusses covered by corrugated metal sheeting.

Climatic considerations largely determined the building's form and materials, but its spaces also have symbolic significance: the school is raised from the ground like the traditional granaries, while the covered areas between the class-rooms evoke the traditional *zandi*. The walls are articulated with pilasters for further structural soundness and to provide solar protection from the east and the west. Shutters running the length of the walls provide ample natural light and ventilation. Climatic comfort is also ensured by the overhanging roof, which shades the façades, by the raising of the corrugated metal roof on a steel truss, allowing cooling air to flow freely between the roof and the ceiling, and through the use of earth blocks for the walls, which absorb heat, moderating room temperature. Details such as the location and scale of blackboards and desks and the rounded edges of the pillars show concern for the safety of children.

Earth for the blocks came from the village itself and was cast in hand presses on site by villagers trained through LOCOMAT. Stabilized compressed earth was also used for the hexagonal paving tiles. In the classrooms, the floors are of rammed earth stabilized with cement. Use of industrial materials was kept to a minimum: the foundations are of stone and poured concrete, and reinforced concrete was used only for the beams that support the ceilings.

Structural use of wood was rejected because there is no local tradition of building in wood and hence little expertise in carpentry, and because native hardwood is scarce and vulnerable to termites. Steel was therefore used for shutters and doors, utilizing a technology with which local craftsmen are familiar. This exigency also suggested the use of steel for the roof, while the roof form was dictated by other practical considerations: it was not possible to transport large elements to the site from afar, nor economically viable to use such lifting machinery as cranes. Instead, the architect devised a process whereby common construction steel bars were cut to predetermined lengths, bent in the middle to form an inverted V, and welded in long modules that could easily be lifted to the top of the building  and tied to the transverse beams. Steel bars running lengthways were welded to these modules in order to tie them together, and corrugated metal sheeting laid on top. All that was necessary was to teach people how to use a handsaw and a small welding machine.

The six houses for teachers and their families are disposed in a wide arc that marks the southern limits of the school site.  Barrel vaults of stabilized earth brick were used for roofs, introducing a new typology to the region, but one that makes use of local resources and is climatically efficient. The choice of siting and the curvilinear site plan work well in the ensemble and evoke the contour of the compounds nearby.

Ancillary services have been built between the school and the teachers' houses, including a toilet block, made in concrete and provided by the Danish Agency for Development Assistance (DANIDA), and a kitchen,  which served as the training prototype for the vaults used in the housing complex. Water was originally carried from a source 7 kilometres away, but a new well, partially sponsored by DANIDA, has simplified their task enormously. A vegetable garden has been set out and trees and shrubs planted alongside the school.

The final form of the new school creates a striking but appropriate presence within the landscape. The combination of a modern architectural language with traditional materials, and of thick brick walls with a floating, almost ethereal, trussed roof, has produced a building that is comfortable to use and sustainable, but also elegant in form. Apart from the training staff from LOCOMAT and the blacksmiths, all the people involved in the construction and project management, including the architect, were native to the village. This group of 150 people, mostly young men but also women and children, proved to be capable of executing structures that were of relative complexity and alien to their building methods, such as the metal trusses of the school building or the barrel vaults in the teachers' houses. The skills learned here can be applied to further initiatives in the village, and might also help secure a future in the construction trade elsewhere.

The way the community organized itself has set an example for two neighbouring villages, which have built their own schools as a cooperative effort. The local authorities have also recognized the project's worth: not only have they provided and paid for the teaching staff, but they have also endeavoured to employ the young people trained here in the town's public projects, using the same techniques. The school was originally intended to serve only the children of Gando, but use by children from neighbouring villages is increasing and, while the school currently houses 150 pupils, it is possible that additional classrooms will be added in the future. Communal spirit is shown in the acceptance of these children,  who reside with various families throughout Gando. Teachers also find that children are more attentive at the Gando school than they are in other schools. Last, but not least, the project has had a positive effect on the community's confidence and earned respect from its neighbours.

**Gando Primary School
Gando, Burkina Faso**

Client
The community of Gando Village, Burkina Faso.

Sponsor
Schulbausteine für Gando e.V. – Bricks
for the Gando School, Germany.

Architect
Diébédo Francis Kéré, Burkina Faso.

Site Coordination
Wénéyda Kéré, Burkina Faso.

Craftsmen
Sanfo Saidou ('Baba') and Oussmane Moné,
master masons; Minoungou Saidou, welder
(all from Burkina Faso).

Consultant
Issa Moné, technical officer, LOCOMAT,
Burkina Faso, training in brick production.

Commission	1998
Design	1999–2000
Construction	October 2000–July 2001
Occupation	October 2001
Site area	30,000m^2
Built area	526m^2
Cost	CFA Francs 22,750,000
	(US$29,830)

Diébédo Francis Kéré (b. 1965, Burkina Faso)
is a member of a family that has represented
village traditions for several centuries. After
receiving training and working as a carpenter
in his country's capital, Ouagadougou, he won
a scholarship from the German government
in 1985 and studied in Germany to become a
development technician. He then studied
architecture under the tutorship of Professor
Peter Herrle, and graduated from Berlin Technical
University in May 2004. During his studies, he
established in Germany Schulbausteine für
Gando, a not-for-profit association, to raise
funds for the Gando Primary School. He has
written numerous articles in German on architecture and development issues in Africa.
Gando Primary School is his first built project.
He is now teaching as an assistant at Berlin
Technical University and continues to present
his experience at international seminars
and conferences.

Website
Schulbausteine für Gando e.V
www.fuergando.de

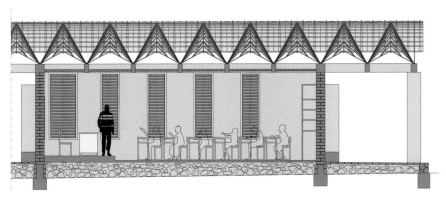

section

1   roof
2   suspended *banco* ceiling
3   concrete beams
4   load-bearing *banco* walls
5   *banco* pilasters
6   steel frames and shutters
7   stone and concrete ramp
8   concrete foundation
9   *banco* shuttering
10 clay and stone infill
11 rammed earth floor
12 stone edging
13 *banco* floor tiles
14 drain

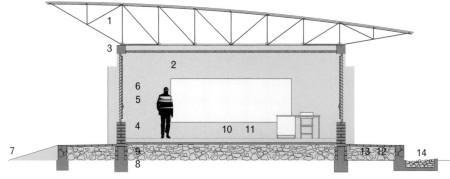

section

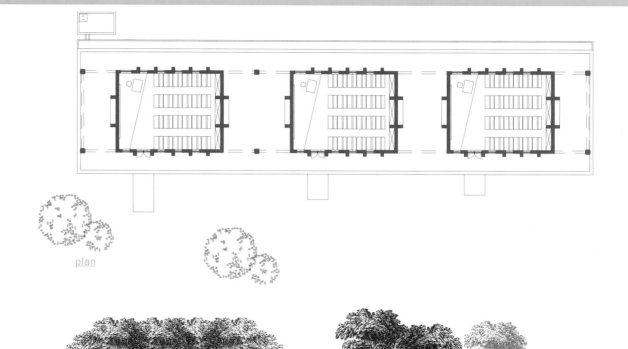

plan

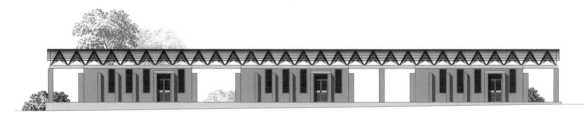

elevation

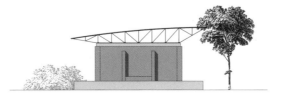

elevation

elevation

elevation

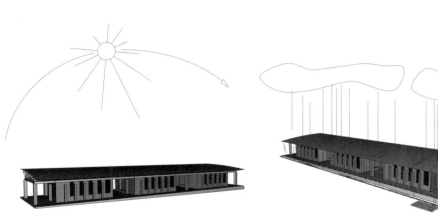

response to climate

47

Iran

India

Mexico

Brazil

Chile

Sandbag Shelter Prototypes

Siberia

Canada

United States

Thailand

The global need for housing includes 17 million refugees and displaced persons – victims of natural disasters and wars. Iranian architect Nader Khalili believes that this need can be addressed only by using the potential of earth construction. After extensive research into vernacular earth building methods in Iran followed by detailed prototyping, he has developed the sandbag or 'superadobe' system. The concept allows people to build their own shelter simply by packing whatever earth they find in their location into sandbags, which are then stacked into dome forms, held together by barbed wire. The shelters are structurally strong – able to resist earthquakes, fires, floods and hurricanes. They are extremely quick, easy and cheap to build. They can be made into permanent structures by rendering them with external plaster and adding any necessary ancillary spaces. They are sustainable in terms of energy, using only sun, shade and gravity. They are adaptable in terms of size, material and configuration, and the system can also be used to build roads and other infrastructure.

These shelters focus on the economic empowerment of people by enabling them to participate in the creation of their own homes and communities. The result is sustainable developments that integrate traditional building materials with modern materials and technology, providing comfortable living spaces acceptable to modern safety standards.

These shelters serve as a prototype for temporary housing using extremely inexpensive means to provide safe homes that can be built quickly and have the high insulation values necessary in arid climates. Their curved form was devised in response to seismic conditions, ingeniously using sand or earth as raw materials, since their flexibility allows the construction of single- and double-curvature compression shells that can withstand lateral seismic forces.

The prototype is a symbiosis of tradition and technology. It employs vernacular forms, integrating load-bearing and tensile structures, but provides a remarkable degree of strength and durability for this type of construction, which is traditionally weak and fragile, through a composite system of sandbags and barbed wire. Created by packing local earth into bags, which are then stacked vertically, the structures are not external systems applied to a territory, but instead grow out of their context, recycling available resources for the provision of housing. The sustainability of this approach is further strengthened because the construction of the sandbag shelters does not require external intervention but can be implemented by the occupants themselves with minimal training. The system is also highly flexible: the scale of structures and arrangement of clusters can be varied and applied to different ecosystems to produce settlements that are suitable for different numbers of individuals or groups with differing social needs. Due to their strength, the shelters can also be made into permanent housing, transforming the outcome of natural disasters into new opportunities.

Architect Nader Khalili started his career as a modernist and achieved success building conventional high-rises. But in 1975 he closed his offices in Los Angeles and Tehran and set out alone by motorcycle into the deserts of his native Iran, convinced that the only way the world's poor could ever afford homes was to build with earth and fire. He dedicated his time to researching traditional vernacular mud construction in Iran and began to work on ideas for using earth as a modern building material. As well as developing a concept for a 'Ceramic House' constructed from sun-dried mud and then fired, Khalili also developed 'Superadobe' – a structure made from sandbags secured with barbed wire. The basic construction technique involves filling sandbags with earth and laying them in courses in a circular plan. The circular courses are corbelled near the top to form a dome. Barbed wire is laid between courses to prevent the sandbags from shifting and to provide earthquake resistance. Hence the materials of war – sandbags and barbed wire – are used for peaceful ends, integrating traditional earth architecture with contemporary global safety requirements.

Using this technology, several design prototypes of domes and vaults were built and tested, including emergency shelters for refugees and the homeless, a sustainable small house called 'Eco-Dome', and a conventionally planned four-bedroom home using a three-vault design concept. The system is particularly suitable for providing temporary shelter because it is cheap and allows buildings to be quickly erected by hand by the occupants themselves with a minimum of training.

Khalili found inspiration for the technology and design of the structures in the principles of Sufi philosophy and Iranian architecture: the unity of the elements of earth, water, air and fire; harnessing sustainable energy – sun, shade, gravity; geometry and symmetry; and the unity of tension and compression. Each shelter comprises one major domed space with some ancillary spaces for cooking and sanitary services. The system is extremely flexible. The earthen materials of clay and sand with straw and water that have been used to make traditional sun-dried mudbricks for millennia are not always available, nor do those most in need of a home have the time to make blocks, dry them and store them. By filling bags directly from the land and reinforcing them with barbed wire, occupants can use almost any earth and the speed of building is much faster. The structures can be temporary or can be made permanent by adding a layer of mud daub or other finishing. Incremental additions such as ovens and animal shelters can also be made to provide a more permanent status, and the accommodation can be tailored to individual needs. The technology can also be used for both buildings and infrastructure such as roads, kerbs, retaining walls and landscaping elements.

The system employs the timeless forms of arches, domes and vaults to create single and double-curvature shell structures that are both strong and aesthetically pleasing. While these load-bearing or compression forms refer to the ancient mudbrick architecture of the Middle East, the use of barbed wire as a tensile element alludes to the portable tensile structures of nomadic cultures. The result is an extremely safe structure. The addition of barbed wire to the compression structures creates earthquake resistance; the aerodynamic form resists hurricanes; the use of sandbags aids flood resistance; and the earth itself provides fireproofing.

The earth used to fill the sandbags is taken from the site where shelters are required and comprises at least 90 per cent of the filling material, although stabilizers such as cement, lime and asphalt emulsion may be added. The barbed wire is four-point, two-strand, galvanized barbed wire and is recyclable. Materials research has shown that the majority of existing bags made of natural or synthetic material can be used. The ideal is a synthetic, ultraviolet-resistant, degradable material. In a temporary building, the bags are allowed to degrade and the building returns to earth.

Because the structures use local resources – on-site earth and human hands – they are entirely sustainable. Men and women, old and young, can build using a can to pour earth. Barbed wire and sandbags are supplied locally, and the stabilizer is also usually locally sourced. The shelters are also sustainable and efficient in energy terms: the wind and the sun provide passive cooling and heating and the sandbags provide thick walls that resist changes in temperature.

Since 1982, Nader Khalili has developed and tested the Super-adobe prototype in California. He has lectured widely on the concept, and presented his ideas at NASA's first Lunar Habitat Symposium in 1984, where he proposed construction with lunar soil. In 1991 he founded the California Institute of Earth Art and Architecture (Cal-Earth), a non-profit research and educational organization that covers everything from construction on the moon and on Mars to housing design and development for the world's homeless for the United Nations. Cal-Earth focuses on researching, developing and teaching the technologies of Superadobe. The intense desert environment of California, with summer temperatures regularly exceeding 40°C and harsh winters with snow and freezing temperatures, flash floods, high winds, and the most dangerous seismic zone in the United States, has provided an ideal testing ground.

The prototypes have not only received California building permits but have also met the requirements of the United Nations High Commissioner for Refugees (UNHCR) for emergency housing. Both the UNHCR and the United Nations Development Programme have chosen to apply the system, which they used in 1995 to provide temporary shelters for a flood of refugees coming into Iran from Iraq.

Throughout the period of prototype building and testing, Khalili's educational philosophy has continued to develop. A distance-teaching programme is being tested for the live broadcast of hands-on instruction directly from Cal-Earth. Many individuals have been trained at Cal-Earth to build with these techniques and are carrying this knowledge to those in need in many countries of the world, from Mongolia to Mexico, India to the United States, and Iran, Brazil, Siberia, Chile and South Africa.

Sandbag Shelter Prototypes
Various locations

Architect
Cal-Earth Institute, US: Nader Khalili, concept and design; Iliona Outram, Project Manager.

Consultants
P. J. Vittore Ltd, US, and C.W. Howe Associates, US, structural engineers.

Sponsors and clients
National Endowment for the Arts, US; Southern California Institute of Architecture (Sci Arc), US; the Ted Turner Foundation, US; United Nations Development Programme (UNDP), US and Switzerland; United Nations High Commissioner for Refugees (UNHCR), Iran offices; the Bureau for Alien and Foreign Immigrant Affairs (BAFIA), Iran; Laura Huxley's Our Ultimate Investment Foundation, US; the Rex Foundation, US; Kit Tremaine, US; the Leventis Foundation, Cyprus; the Flora Family Foundation, US.

Prototypes built to date
Hamid Irani and Iraqi refugees at Baninajar Camp, Iran; Eric Hansen, Mexico; Djalal and Shahla Sherafat, Canada; Michelle Queyroy and orphans at the MEG Foundation, India; Dada Krpasundarananda, India, Thailand and Siberia; Mara Cranic, Baja, Mexico; Virginia Sanchis, Brazil; Patricio Calderon, Chile; Jim Guerra and Mexican farmworkers, US; Don Graber, Craig Cranic, Giovanni Panza and Yacqui People of Sarmiento, Mexico.

Timetable
Sandbag Shelters (Superadobe): first development, 1992.

Nader Khalili (b. 1937, Iran) trained as an architect in Iran, Turkey and the United States. From 1970 to 1975, he practised architecture in Iran, and has since dedicated himself to research into building with earth. He has served as a consultant to the United Nations (UNIDO) and a contributor to NASA. In 1991, Mr Khalili founded the California Institute of Earth Art and Architecture (Cal-Earth) in Hesperia, US, and he teaches architectural research at Sci Arc. He has received awards from organizations such as the California chapter of the American Institute of Architects, for 'Excellence in Technology'; the United Nations and HUD (US Department of Housing and Urban Development), for 'Shelter for the Homeless'; and the American Society of Civil Engineers (Aerospace Division), for his work in lunar-base-building technology. He is the author of five published books, including two translations of the work of the thirteenth-century Sufi poet, Jalal-e-Din Mohammad Rumi.

Website
Cal-Earth
www.calearth.org

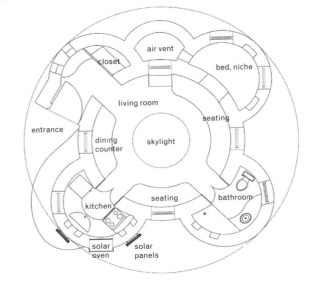

floor plan

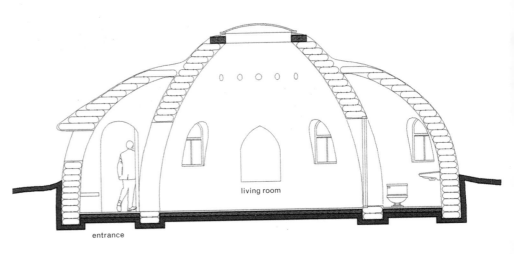

section 1

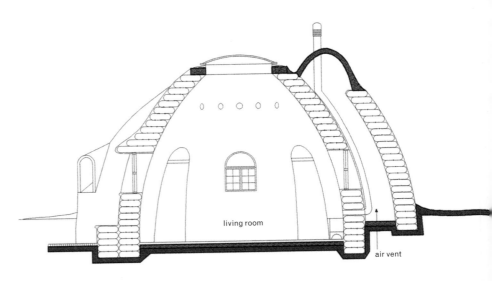

section 2

58

Asnaf, Yemen

Restoration of Al-Abbas Mosque

Al-Abbas Mosque is a testimony to the living traditions and architectural achievements of one of the world's earliest civilizations. Built over 800 years ago, the mosque is situated on the remains of a pre-Islamic shrine or temple on a site honoured as a sacred place since ancient times. Its cubic form also has ancient precedents, including the Kaaba in Mecca.

The mosque is noted for its exceptionally fine ceiling, carved, gilded and painted in masterful style. The local population, proud members of a tribal society, continues to revere the mosque and the site today still holds special significance for them. Tribesmen often gather here for the quiet discussion of matters important to them, or the peaceful resolution of conflicts or differences. Villagers living in this remote area use the mosque for prayers, and local women visit the tomb of the holy figure after whom the mosque is named.

By the mid-1980s, deterioration of some of the timber elements of the painted ceiling had become advanced and portions were beginning to fall off. The ceiling was dismantled and transported to the National Museum in Yemen's capital, Sana'a. Local outcry at this removal initiated the restoration of the mosque itself and reinstallation of the original ceiling.

The project represents a fine example of international and local collaboration to achieve the highest standards of conservation and to enable the training of Yemeni experts, who are now continuing the use of these techniques. More importantly, it represents the determination and success of a local community in reclaiming this important example of architectural heritage as an integral, essential part of their contemporary lives.

Asnaf

This scheme has been chosen to receive an Award because it applies exemplary conservation standards and engages local pride in safeguarding this culturally significant monument for future generations.

The project represents the establishment of a successful and sustainable partnership between local and external expertise for the conservation process. Although the restoration spanned approximately ten years during exceptional political conditions, the consistency, dedication and commitment of both the external and local stakeholders ensured that the fabric of the building was not compromised in any way. In fact, the process has raised the benchmark for restoration in the region, reviving traditional practices in tandem with modern scientific approaches to conservation. These range from the use of traditional mortars and plasters to complex structural repairs and the conservation of the delicate decorative ceiling paintings.

The project also demonstrates sensitivity in dealing with the building as a living fabric. The restoration has extended the significance and usefulness of this historic mosque for the benefit of the larger social, cultural and physical landscape in which it is situated.

Set in the highlands of Yemen, 40 kilometres from Sana'a, Al-Abbas Mosque dates from the turbulent last days before the overthrow of the Sulayhid Dynasty, who ruled Yemen from 1046 to 1137. An inscription in the interior dates the building to Dhu al-Hijjah 519 (December 1125– January 1126 in the Gregorian calendar) and names the founder as Sultan Musa bin Muhammed al-Fitti. Another inscription names the builder or architect as Muhammed ibn Abul-Fath ibn Arhab. But the mosque is in fact named after a little-known figure called 'Abbas', a holy man who is believed to be buried there. The presence of ancient relics dating to the second century AD also suggests that a sacred building existed on the site in pre-Islamic times. The mosque is not only used for prayer by local villagers but also functions as a meeting place where problems between tribes can be resolved, while local women leave votive offerings at the tomb of Abbas.

From its isolated position on the side of a 2,350-metre-high hill  in this volcanic region, the mosque looks over surrounding mountains and valleys and several small villages, the closest being Asnaf, 2 kilometres away. Like the buildings of these local villages, the lower parts of the mosque's walls are made of stone, with mud bricks at the upper levels. Almost square in plan, the mosque has a flat roof, making it cubic in shape. Inside are six columns, four in stone dating from pre-Islamic times and two in brick. Three of the columns have antique capitals. The columns divide the interior into four rows, leading towards the *mihrab* wall.

But the mosque's most important architectural feature is its elaborate coffered ceiling, which is in complete contrast to the building's modest exterior. Most of it has survived intact since its construction, providing an excellent example of the artistic style that flourished in Yemen in the early twelfth century and an important reference for art historians. The ceiling's twenty-two caissons are covered with intricate decoration carved, gilded and painted in tempera on a wooden support. The eighty different geometric and floral motifs that appear on the ceiling are traditional to the area, but also show Sassanid, Fatimid and Ghaznavid influences. The number of steps in each caisson increases towards the *mihrab*, and the caisson directly in front of the *mihrab* has seven steps, signifying the seven layers of heaven. In addition, there is an inscribed frieze around the *mihrab* and a triple-band frieze around the top of the walls that continues the decorative scheme of the ceiling.

By the 1980s, the ceiling was suffering from rot and warping and the number of worshippers at the mosque was beginning to fall. In 1985, the Yemeni Government's General Organization for Antiquities, Museums and Manuscripts asked the French Centre for Yemeni Studies in Sana'a to help preserve the ceiling. In order for the repair to take place, the ceiling was dismantled with funding from UNESCO and removed to the National Museum at Sana'a, where a workshop was established. In 1987 the French Centre asked archaeologist and conservator Marylène Barret to carry out the restoration of the ceiling, which took three years.

For the slow, painstaking process of cleaning the decorated roof panels, a mixture of solvents was applied with cotton swabs, before fixing the decoration with a diltuted resin. The importance of preserving the history of the ceiling was respected. If the original paint had been washed off an area, it was left as it was. If a new board was used, it was either left without any ornamentation or decorated only on one or two ends with watercolour, leaving the middle part unpainted. Some parts of the decoration were left untouched so that the difference between 'before' and 'after' could be seen, and the new watercolour decorations were waterproofed chemically. When a new board was used to replace a carved, painted and gilded horizontal element, it was not carved but painted to create a *trompe-l'oeil* effect. Cracked pieces of wood were reinforced from the back, using old timber wherever possible.

The Gulf War in 1990 and the outbreak of civil war in Yemen in 1994 brought the project to a halt. During this time, fierce opposition to the removal of the mosque's ceiling was voiced by members of the Helwan tribes, who insisted the ceiling be returned to its original location. Before the ceiling could be returned to the mosque, however, it was clear that major repairs would have to be made to the roof, which had a hole in it, and the decision was taken to restore the fabric of the building itself. Marylène Barret was also asked to undertake this work and she called in Yemeni architect Abdullah Al-Hadrami to work with her. These two experts assembled a team of French and Yemeni archaeologists and the best local craftsmen, who worked together to complete the restoration project in 1996.

The principal goal was to restore the building with a minimum of intervention. To achieve this, traditional materials and techniques – many still in use today – were employed wherever possible. No speculative elements were inserted: all new elements can be traced back to original examples in both their form and their location.

Brickwork that had previously been repaired incorrectly was pulled down and the walls bonded with new bricks made in the same way as the originals. Door and window openings that had been blocked were opened up, bringing light into the interior. On the west wall, a window frieze with pre-Islamic motifs was revealed inside the door arch during the cleaning work. On the *mihrab* wall, only a small amount of plaster was replaced; the rest was conserved or repaired. On the other walls, most surfaces were renewed with mud plaster, covered by a top coat of gypsum rubbed with mustard oil to create a patina. The floor was covered with *qudad* – a traditional mortar composed of lime and volcanic aggregate that is polished with a smooth stone and daubed with animal fat. Electricity was installed and, as fragments of alabaster lamps had been found during the repair of the floor, the mosque is now lit by three traditional lamps of this type, with electric bulbs. An ablution tank to the west of the building was also restored and a new stone pavement built around the mosque to aid water drainage.

An attic space 1.2 metres high between the ceiling and the roof would have enabled construction of the original coffered ceiling. Six brick piers supported the roof within this space but these were disintegrating and so were rebuilt. The original roof was then reconstructed, with a layer of thin branches laid across beams, covered with a thick layer of earth and then a final layer of *qudad*. The single rainwater outlet on the original roof was considered insufficient because of the risks that water penetration poses in preservation, so three additional drains were created. Several of the original merlons on the roof were missing, but from six surviving merlons it was possible to tell the exact shape and location of the originals, so that replacements, made from brick like the surviving examples, could be placed correctly.

After the completion of the roof, one thousand separate pieces of ceiling were carefully assembled like a puzzle and numbered in the museum. They were then transported to the mosque, one row at a time, and fixed to an ingenious new supporting structure of U-shaped box beams that is entirely hidden now that the restored panels are in place.

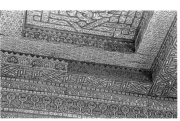

Since the restoration, the building's original elegance and decoration have come alive, increasing the interest of the local residents, who are proud of their mosque and are especially happy to see the beautiful ceiling back in place. The restoration of the mosque is also of great significance for the history of architecture: Al-Abbas Mosque is an important historical record that reflects artistic, social, cultural and economic values in this part of the world dating from the early twelfth century back to pre-Islamic times. To preserve such a building is an important way of inspiring future generations to understand their own culture and claim possession of it. In addition, the restoration principles employed in Al-Abbas Mosque may well serve as a guide for further projects concerned with the preservation of cultural property, and the project may stimulate further research, particularly in relation to a number of ruins surrounding the mosque site. The restoration of Al-Abbas Mosque is a testament to the cooperation of the local and foreign experts who brought the project to fruition.

**Restoration of Al-Abbas Mosque
Asnaf Village, Khawlan region, Yemen**

Client
Government of Yemen, General Organization
for Antiquities, Museums and Manuscripts,
Yemen: Yussuf Abdallah, Director; Qadi Ismail
Al-Akwa, former Director; French Centre for
Yemeni Studies, Yemen: Jean Lambert, Director;
Frank Mermier and Rémy Audouin, former
directors.

Sponsors
United Nations Educational, Scientific, and
Cultural Organization, France; French Ministry
of Foreign Affairs, General Directorate of
Cultural, Scientific and Technical Relations,
Archaeology Department, France: Philippe
Georgeais, Director; Jean-Claude Jacq and
Philippe Guillemin, former directors.

Conservators
Marylène Barret, France, conservator and
coordinator, with assistance from Abdullah
Al-Hadrami, Yemen, for architectural and
masonary restoration.

Restorers
Ceiling and woodwork: François de Bazelaire,
France, and Benoit Cruypennick, France, wood
restorers; Gilbert Delcroix, France, advisor;
Camilia An'am, Abeer Radwan, Khalida Hassan,
Adel Said, Rashad al Kubati, and Mohamed al
Noman, archaeologists (all from Yemen);
Samia Noman, Yemen, archivist.

Masonary
Mohamed Satar, master builder; Ahmed al
Arasi, *qudad* work; Ahmet al Tairi and Mohamed
al Namrani, gypsum work; Ali al Imad, master
mason; Mohammed al Siry, master carpenter
(all from Yemen).

Master craftsman and caretaker
Ahmed Al-Shadhabi, Yemen.

Commission   1986
Design   1987–May 1992
Construction   December 1995–March 1996
Occupation   May 1996

Site area   1200m²
Built area   110m²

Cost   US$400,000

The French Centre for Yemeni Studies (Centre
Français d'Études Yémenites – CFEY) initiates,
coordinates and supports the work of French,
Yemeni and foreign teams in the fields of social
sciences and archaeology in Yemen and
neighbouring countries (Oman, Saudi Arabia
and Eritrea). Established in 1982, the centre is
administered by the General Directorate of
Cultural, Scientific and Technical Relations of
the French Ministry of Foreign Affairs, which
also funds its activities. Marylène Barret (b. 1954,
France) was trained as an archaeologist at the
Sorbonne and at the École du Louvre in Paris.
Specializing in the restoration of wall paintings,
she has worked in France and Italy as well as
Syria, Jordan, Morocco, Tunisia and Pakistan,
in addition to her continuing work in Yemen.
Abdallah Al-Hadrami (b. 1957, Yemen) is an
architect and specialist in conservation who
graduated from the New York Institute of
Technology. He has been a contributor to
most major conservation projects in Yemen
since 1990 as the Director General of the
Department of Technical Cooperation at the
General Organization for Protection of Historic
Cities of Yemen. He received an Aga Khan Award
in 1995 for his contribution to the conservation of
the Old City of Sana'a.

Website
French Centre for Yemeni Studies
www.univ-aix.fr/cefas/

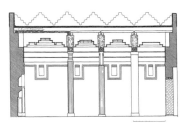

cross section

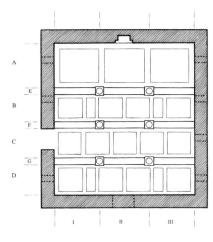

plan of mosque

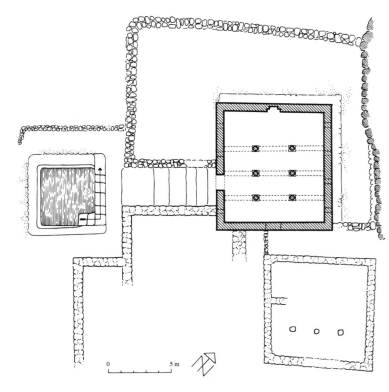

site plan of mosque, ablution tank and ruins

A

B

C

D

plans and sections of caissons

floral and geometric motifs

Old City, Jerusalem

Old City of Jerusalem Revitalization Programme

Jerusalem has an extraordinarily long and varied history, but the urban fabric of the old city is threatened by overcrowding, lack of maintenance and poor services. The Old City of Jerusalem Revitalization Programme aims to rehabilitate the city, to preserve its heritage and to create a better quality of life for its inhabitants. It is a comprehensive project aimed at every aspect of human life, with several components, including restoration, training, education and raising public awareness. All these components are tied together to achieve an integrated and enduring revitalization. The restoration work is undertaken in compliance with internationally accepted principles, using traditional methods and materials. The body of completed works to date includes over 160 projects, all undertaken in close collaboration with local institutions, international organizations and funding agencies.

The programme has created decent living conditions through the restoration of traditional dwellings. It has provided social, cultural and recreational services for the community. It has created a network of national and international organizations involved in conservation of built heritage. And the workings of the programme will allow for the wider dissemination of information and experience to interested professionals and the public. All this has been achieved through safeguarding the cultural property of a World Heritage city.

The programme has received an Award for its comprehensive approach towards sustaining the life of a community in its natural setting – a life threatened by the deterioration of its physical, social and economic conditions.

The project is successful in addressing several issues, including the restoration and rehabilitation of housing, as well as the adaptive reuse of historic buildings and monuments for new functions. The programme is notable for the training it provides in conservation for architects, engineers, contractors and craftspeople, and for its intention to establish an information centre and a database for the old city, including documentation, surveys, research and studies. Finally, the project has created a community outreach programme to raise public awareness of the value of historic buildings and to encourage public participation in the process of rehabilitation and restoration.

This effort is conducted under severe constraints, restoring the old city as a living, vibrant and beautiful environment. The process is meticulously conducted by a team of professionals motivated by their love of the place and its people. This is a project about dignity and self-esteem.

Jerusalem has been continuously inhabited since the fourth millennium BC. It has come under Persian, Greek, Roman, Byzantine, Fatimid, Mamluk, Ottoman and British rule and is of key importance for the Jewish, Christian and Islamic faiths. The old city – surrounded by walls built by the Ottoman Sultan Süleyman the Magnificent in the sixteenth century – is divided into Arab, Jewish and Christian quarters and over 90 per cent of the 31,000 people living there are Palestinian. The urban fabric has, however, suffered from neglect, inappropriate use and inadequate services, with many people living in dilapidated buildings in unsanitary conditions. This situation was exacerbated in 1995 when natives of Jerusalem who were living outside the city were required by Israeli law to reside in the city in order to keep their Jerusalem identification papers. This resulted in a sudden increase in the population of the old city and chronic overcrowding; living conditions became almost impossible.

The situation forced residents to extreme measures, including flattening roofs by removing vaults and domes in order to expand vertically, often using materials that are incompatible with the original architecture. In many cases kitchen and toilet facilities were shared by a number of families and water, drainage and sewage connections were often badly installed, resulting in leakage and contributing to health and environmental problems.

To address these issues the Welfare Association – a Geneva-based non-governmental organization set up in 1983 to support Palestinians in all development areas – set up a technical office in Jerusalem in 1995. The office is composed of professionals from different fields: architecture, engineering, planning, economics and history. Its main aim is to implement a comprehensive programme for the rehabilitation of the old city, comprising a number of complementary components: a revitalization plan; emergency restoration; total restoration; training in conservation; and a community outreach programme.

The Old City Revitalization Plan forms the basis of the programme's work. A broad survey was carried out to identify the buildings most in danger and make proposals for their rehabilitation. The aim is not the immediate restoration of a contiguous quarter but interventions throughout the old city. The buildings might be houses – either single buildings of two or three storeys housing one or two families, or traditional residential complexes (*hosh*) of several units surrounding a courtyard and housing up to ten families. The programme also focuses on major public or religious buildings – mosques, churches, *madrasas* (schools), hostels – some of which retain their original function, while others are adapted to a new use. The programme is concerned with the preservation of the whole of the old city, not just the Arab quarter, and projects have been undertaken in the Christian quarter.

A number of factors are considered in identifying projects for rehabilitation, including the physical and structural condition of the buildings, their historical and architectural significance, legal ownership and social, economic and political factors. Buildings are selected for either emergency or total restoration. Emergency restoration is normally a quick and limited intervention to solve particularly urgent problems that pose immediate health or safety risks, such as structural instability or water leakage. However, the programme often tries to implement additional improvements while dealing with such problems. The budget for such interventions varies depending on the nature of the work, from US$4,500 to US$60,000.

A greater number of buildings require total restoration. In each of these, structural problems are resolved and new finishes and fittings are installed. Inappropriate additions are removed and replaced, if necessary, with lightweight new structures using modern materials. In accordance with international conservation standards, such additions are reversible. Areas that cannot be removed are masked by rough plaster with a wash the colour of stone.

The programme also follows international standards in using only original traditional building materials and methods: the rubble-stone vaults and walls are plastered with lime, and original old stone floors are maintained and reapplied – methods that are climatically appropriate and well-known locally. No new openings are allowed nor any additions that might affect original walls, floors, ceilings or roofs. As much as possible, the restorers refrain from using cement.

In restoring houses, the programme recognizes the vernacular character of the structures and adopts a pragmatic approach that is sensitive to the needs of the users and allows them flexibility, rather than imposing a new way of life. Each family is provided with a separate kitchen, bathroom and toilet, as well as basic services such as heating for water, a sink and a counter in the kitchen, where the walls and floor are tiled. The electricity, water and sewage systems are updated or installed, as appropriate. The designers and builders also show great ingenuity in improvising elements that are unavailable or unaffordable, such as light fixtures and railings. The cost of total restoration projects is much higher than emergency ones, ranging between US$65,000 and US$2,715,000.

One of the biggest problems the team faces is that beneficiaries continue to use buildings during the restoration work or need to return to them as soon as possible. Finding alternative accommodation is very difficult and costly, particularly for residents. Therefore, the team tries to organize and manage the various tasks to allow for continuing use of buildings. Another major issue is the provision of kitchens and bathrooms for each family in buildings where there is no room to spare. In such cases the services are often constructed in a courtyard, as at the Hosh Helou, where a large, multi-levelled courtyard was arranged, providing a shared open space for the families that live there. Below the courtyard of the Hosh Gheith a previously unknown space dating from the Crusader period was discovered, restored and utilized.

The duration of the projects varies from about three months for a small house to many years for non-residential projects such as the area called Burj al Laqlaq, which was begun in 1996 and is still ongoing. Providing one of the very few large open spaces in the walled old city, Burj al Laqlaq is a community project dedicated to children. It has a playground, a football field, which can be used for other purposes, and a nursery. A temporary tent is also planned for youth camps. Dar al Aytam also focuses on young people. This historical orphanage, which comprises five monumental buildings from the Mamluk and Ottoman periods – including a soup kitchen and bakery established by the wife of Sultan Süleyman – is being upgraded incrementally as an educational institution. Work on buildings of such historic and architectural value is carried out slowly and sensitively and decisions are made with great care.

The other areas of the programme complement the restoration work to ensure the sustainability of the improvements. The restoration work has created an important new market for architectural firms and contractors and the training programme aims to establish standards and guidelines in the field of restoration to be followed by all those involved. Training for architects, engineers, contractors and craftspeople is provided through short courses, internships and fellowships to study abroad.

A community outreach programme raises public awareness of the value of historic buildings and encourages public participation in the rehabilitation process. As well as creating a sense of community, the outreach programme organizes publications, meetings, workshops and lectures for schools, religious organizations, residents and users.

Two further components of the programme are also proposed. Firstly, an information centre will provide documentation and publications relating to the programme's work, and a data bank of conservation professionals and organizations. Secondly, the Jerusalem Institute for the Preservation of Architectural Heritage in Palestine will offer courses for training and capacity building, and is intended to raise standards of conservation in Palestine by strengthening contacts with similar organizations.

In addition to the eighteen staff of the technical office, those working on the programme include a large number of visiting experts and consultants from a range of professions, based in Palestine or abroad. The labour force and contractors are Palestinians from Jerusalem or nearby. They often have problems entering the city because of the political situation and this sometimes stops work on the projects. While the technical office is responsible for implementing the overall programme, it works in close cooperation with other organizations for both the restoration work and the training programme, such as the United Nations Educational, Scientific and Cultural Organization (UNESCO) and the International Centre for the Study of the Preservation and Restoration of Cultural Property (ICCROM). Funding has been provided by the Welfare Association, the Arab Fund for Economic and Social Development, the Islamic Development Bank, the Arab Fund and the Ford Foundation among others.

By the end of 2003, eighty-two residential projects and twenty-six public and fifty-five commercial buildings had been restored through the programme, providing decent living conditions for residents, creating new spaces for the community and ensuring the preservation of the rich historic fabric of the old city. A spirit of friendly interaction with the inhabitants has been maintained through continuous dialogue with those affected, and the beneficiaries are happy with the improvements. The reaction of local institutions is positive and many groups have expressed their readiness to assist. The programme has created jobs for professionals and labourers, boosting the economy of the old city, and has also trained large numbers of people, including builders and craftspeople. The success of the programme has been ensured through a cooperative spirit, which is visible in its internal management, its relationship to its clients and its interaction with other agencies, both local and international. In difficult political circumstances, the programme is well organized and strives for the highest international standards. Its objectives are implemented not only with professionalism but also with dedication and zeal. With its carefully planned and integrated components, the Old City of Jerusalem Revitalization Programme is an example for all similar endeavours, and one that generates hope.

Old City of Jerusalem Revitalization Programme (OCJRP)
Old City, Jerusalem

Project principals
Welfare Association, Switzerland: Hisham
Qaddumi, Jordan, Chairman of the Technical
Committee of the OCJRP; Ismael El-Zabri,
Jordan, Director General; Shadia Touqan,
Jerusalem, Director of the OCJRP Technical
Office.

Partners
Department of Islamic Waqf, Jerusalem; Division
of Cultural Heritage, United Nations Educational,
Scientific, and Cultural Organization, France.

Sponsors
Arab Fund for Economic and Social Develop-
ment, Kuwait; Islamic Development Bank,
Saudi Arabia; the Ford Foundation, US.

Project team
Ehab Zuheaka, Deputy Director; Khalid Halabi,
Supervision Unit Manager; Amal Abu Al-Hawa,
Samer Rantisi, Sahar Ghazal, Bashar Husseini,
Faten Lafi, Bahi Abdel Hadi, Marah El-Aloui and
Nisreen Karsou, architects; Khaled Muhanna,
Lana El-Khushashi and Suhad Al-Bakri, civil
engineers; Hazem Quneibi and Wafa Elder,
administration; Arda Batarseh, information
manager; Yousef Natche, architectural historian;
Anita Vitullo, editor (all based in Jerusalem).

Consultants
Instituto Veneto per i Beni Culturali, Italy,
2002–present; Riwaq Centre for Architectural
Conservation, Ramallah: Suad Al-Amiri,
Director, 1998–2000; Centre for Conservation and
Preservation of Islamic Architectural Heritage,
Egypt: Saleh Lamei Mostafa, Director, 1997–98.

Commission	July 1994
Design	1995–ongoing
Construction	1995–ongoing
Occupation	Since 1996
Site area	871,000m² old city
Cost	US$12,382,000 (1996–2003)

The Welfare Association is a private, non-
profit foundation established in 1983 in Geneva,
Switzerland, to support sustainable development
in Palestinian societies. The association is better
known by its Arabic name, Ta'awoun, which means
cooperation. As part of its efforts, the Welfare
Association established a special technical unit
in 1995 dedicated to the revitalization of the old
city of Jerusalem through rehabilitation of
housing and related services, preservation of
cultural, historical and religious monuments and
improvement of living standards for residents of
the old city. The technical team of the OICJRP is
composed of eight architects and engineers and
ten support staff led by Shadia Touqan (b. 1947,
Nablus), an architect and urban planner with over
thirty years of experience in the field of architecture and urban conservation.

Website
Welfare Association
www.welfareassociation.org

stylistic periods

- Raman
- Byzantine
- Umayyad
- Abbasid
- Fatimid
- Crusader
- Ayyubid
- Mamluk
- Early Ottoman
- Late Ottoman
- British Mandate
- 1948-1967
- Post 1967
- No Data

current use

- Residential
- Religious
- Commercial
- Public
- Closed
- Archeological Site
- No Data

physical condition

- Very Good
- Good
- Satisfactory
- Bad
- No Data

structural condition

- Very Good
- Good
- Satisfactory
- Bad
- No Data

additions

- Horizontal
- Vertical
- Horizontal Vertical
- No Additions OR No Data

building heights

- One Story/Level
- Two Stories/Levels
- Three Stories/Levels
- Four Stories/Levels
- Five Stories/Levels
- No Data

floors

- Stone Tiles
- Carpet Tiles
- Ceramic Tiles
- Cement Tiles
- Cement
- Mud
- No Data

ceilings

- Cross Vaulted
- Barrel Vaulted
- Domed
- Level
- Level with iron supports (I Section)
- Wood
- No Data

roofs

- Level
- Pitched
- Domed
- No Data

Ayvacık, Turkey

B2 House

Two Turkish brothers, Selman and Suha Bilal, wanted to build a house on Turkey's north Aegean coast as a place to spend weekends in a spot where they could find beauty, tranquillity and seclusion without travelling long distances from their homes in Istanbul. They approached Turkish architect Han Tümertekin, who conceived the idea of creating a refuge for these two widely travelled urbanite 'nomads', as he describes them, whose relationship to place is transitory and who seek privacy in the openness of spectacular landscapes. The pure rectangular mass of the house sits on an open terraced site, unmistakably modern and separate from the traditional houses of the surrounding village, but respecting and allying itself with those houses through its use of traditional local materials and techniques. These are combined with contemporary architectural elements with utter simplicity. The materials and structure are expressed openly and left unadorned to create a house of resonant austerity. The house opens itself to its surroundings and encourages its users not only to observe the landscape but also to immerse themselves in nature through the use of semi-external and external parts of the accommodation. It is a place where a basic shelter becomes a space for the celebration and contemplation of nature.

B2 House

This house has been chosen to receive an Award because it embodies a sense of perfection and well-being. It represents a progressive approach in acknowledging the history of its place, the surrounding houses and landscape, to form a new and unique creation that is, at the same time, an integral part of its community. The house stands apart – beautifully shaped and elegantly dressed – but in the future additional houses may embrace and adopt it, fully integrating it into a wider landscape.

B2 conveys a maximum amount of dignity, achieved with a minimum of means. It celebrates the act of contemplation, looking towards the distant horizon with openness and clarity. It incorporates a wealth of architectural knowledge but at the same time expresses the individuality of the architect's aspirations.

When filled with life and activity, the house becomes a place of special significance and reference in the community, embracing all those whom it welcomes as visitors or passers-by. When empty, it continues to command the respect it so much deserves.

B2 House is located on the edges of Büykhüsun, a small village  near Ayvacik in an area of great historical and archaeological interest that is relatively underdeveloped. Its cluster of stone houses ranges down the rocky mountainside, housing a tightly knit community of around 450 people who work mainly in agriculture. The houses are simple rectangular masses constructed entirely of the local granite and volcanic stone, laid in interlocking layers. Located just outside the south-east boundary of the village, B2 House takes its cue from the orientation of the trad-itional houses, with windows placed on the south façade, looking out over spectacular panoramic views of valleys, mountains and the sea, while a northern façade, lower in height, turns its back on the prevailing north-easterly wind.

The architect's response to the sloping topography of the triangular site, which drops 7 metres from north to south, is also based on the local practice of terracing. The site is divided into two flat plateaus with a difference of 1.3 metres between them, creating a long rectangular terrace,  on which the house is placed, and a triangular terrace to the back of the house, which is used as a garden. This means that, like the local houses, B2 House is embedded in the slope of the mountainside. However, in contrast to the local building typology, with houses grouped around small walled gardens to ensure an element of privacy, there are no garden walls around B2 House. As a result, the site is absorbed by the surrounding landscape but, at the same time, the house is set apart, appearing almost as a sculpture on a pedestal.

It was important for the owners to contain the scale of the house in order to limit construction costs while achieving a simple, practical structure that would not demand much maintenance. The programme is therefore basic – anything outside the realm of necessity is omitted – and the house is fairly small. The ground floor is dominated by a large living room and the upper floor by two bedrooms. The connection between the two floors is through an external stair of wood and steel, which rests on the upper terrace, 3 metres from the house, with a deck that bridges to the main structure.

The external stair  not only makes maximum use of the inner spaces of the house and eliminates any element that might distract from their purity, but also integrates nature with one of the typical domestic features of the house: to live there it is necessary to use this exterior stair, which is the sole link between the floors. If the main premise of building this house was to immerse its users in nature, features such as this ensure that their relationship with nature is active and reciprocal, not based solely on the detached process of gazing at the landscape.

The purity of the main spaces and an integration with nature are also maintained by semi-external spaces set within a 1.2-metre-deep utility wall that aligns the north façade and is sealed off from the living area by two frosted-glass sliding doors. Here, accessed through reed-panel doors that cover the two main openings to the house, are bath-rooms, a laundry area, storage, a kitchenette  and a fireplace that opens onto an outdoor living room sheltered beneath the stair deck – an arrangement that serves to emphasize further the importance of outdoor spaces as integral parts of the house.

The structure of the house is fairly simple and was designed with local technology in mind. The idea was to achieve a rigid, monolithic structural box that is able to resist seismic forces, since the area is subject to earthquakes. The east and west façades comprise a tripartite composition consisting of two 1.2-metre-wide concrete structural members that frame a 3.6-metre-wide stone wall. This is continued on the roof, although the stones there are not fixed. The result is a continuous uninterrupted surface that wraps around and defines the mass, appearing to be a single folded plane.

As well as referring to the local houses, the use of stone on the side walls forms a richly textured element, framed by more modern elements. The use of man-made structures to frame a natural material is an important recurring theme throughout the building: the house frames the landscape,  the concrete structure frames the stone walls and, in the folding panels that shade the southern façade, aluminium frames reed.

One of the architect's concerns was to provide a design that could be easily constructed by local builders. The architect devised a framework that the local builders could implement without much guidance, minimizing the number of site visits and ensuring a high quality of execution. For example, work that required heavy super-vision, such as building the concrete structure, was separated from work that required less, such as the stone work. As a result, despite its modern appearance, the house was mainly built with local technology and materials. Only the glazing system used on the southern façade and for the sliding doors was brought from Istanbul and installed by the manufacturer.

In its materials the house attempts to bridge the architectural gap between the village and itself through the visual continuity of textures, colours and scale. The result is an ambivalent relationship between house and village, the house's clear autonomy being counteracted by the dialogue it establishes with its built surroundings.

The final appearance of B2 House is a direct expression of its structure and materials and of its construction process. Nothing is concealed. Each material is allowed to express itself clearly. Every component is left bare and unsheathed – a feature described by the architect as 'honesty'. This also has the practical virtue of making the house extremely easy to maintain: only the reed panels must be replaced annually. But where the materials used in the project are generally raw, refinement emerges with their layout and relationship in a scheme of calculated rusticity that is at the same time in no way nostalgic. The flooring of the house is the only instance in which one material is used to cover another. While the ground floor is of terrazzo poured *in situ*, the upper level is finished with wood. These materials relate to the immediate exterior of each level: the terrazzo is conceived as a refined version of the garden, where large, flat pebbles were used as ground cover for the terraces; the wood is an extension of the external stair and wooden deck.

The owners' key concern in constructing B2 House was to be close to nature, and the house is intended to be used as a space for contemplating the surroundings. They are extremely fond of the house and its location and feel that it is conducive to the well-being of its users: 'Even if we spend one day in the house it is sufficient to feel totally rejuvenated.' During the initial design stages they were concerned that the villagers might not like the aesthetic of the house, but the design was approved by the village *muhtar* (administrator) before construction. Upon its completion the owners were relieved to find that the house was admired by the local community, although it is regarded as an object of curiosity and is known as 'the Japanese house'. The social balance of Büykhüsun has not been disturbed by the owners of B2 house, since the local community is quite accepting of newcomers. Indeed, there are twenty holiday houses in the village belonging to outsiders, whose presence is regarded as a positive influence on the economy and land value of the village.

With a reduced architectural language employing humble materials and rudimentary forms, remarkable spatial conditions are achieved in B2 House. The architect has managed to draw uncommon energies from common forms by virtue of siting, organization and thematic consistency. The context of the project becomes a point of reference, subject to editing and reduction, and the house examines traditional architectural notions about property, privacy, domesticity, identity and space, with ground-breaking results.

The treatment of boundaries generates a vast non-private territory that seeps through the spatial structure of the house, expanding its limits towards the horizon. The spaces gain a sublime presence that transforms the sense of a dwelling into that of a monument. The house functions as an apparatus for perceiving nature with truly mesmerizing effects, constantly shifting the user from domestic activity to a state of pure contemplation in a suspended timeless zone. Its capacity to transport its users between different realms extends to its image: the pure mass on a pedestal is conceived with the silent grandeur and noble simplicity of a monument, while its scale and humble materials take it back to the realm of the vernacular.

B2 House
Büykhüsun Village, Ayvacık, Turkey

Clients
Selman and Suha Bilal

Architect
Han Tümertekin, designer; Eylem Erdinç,
Project Architect; Hakan Sengün, Hayriye Sözen
and Ahmet Önder, assistant architects (all based
in Istanbul).

Consultant
Gülsün Parlar, Turkey, structural engineer.

Contractor
Ziya Ildiz, Turkey, Project Coordinator

Craftsman
Enver Akan, Turkey, master builder.

Commission   1999
Design   March 1999–October 1999
Construction   November 1999–April 2001
Occupation   June 2001

Site area   600m^2
Built area   150m^2

Cost   US$140,000

Han Tümertekin (b. 1958, Turkey) graduated
from Istanbul Technical University in 1982.
After working two years in the office of Ahmet
Gülgönen and then at the Atelier d'Architecture
Bernstein-Champetier-Vidal in Paris, he
established the Han Tümertekin-Resit Soley
Partnership in Istanbul. In 1986, he opened his
own practice under the name of Mimarlar Tasarim
Danımanlık Ltd and has designed and built a
number of residential and public buildings in
Turkey. He has twice been awarded Turkey's
National Architecture Award, in 1998 and 2000,
and received the Tepe Centre Architectural
Award in 2000 for two of his projects. He has
been visiting professor at various schools of
architecture in Turkey.

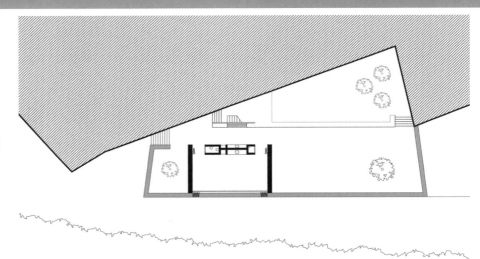

ground floor

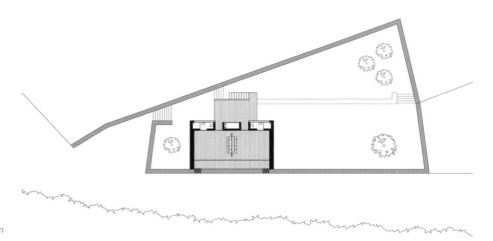

first floor

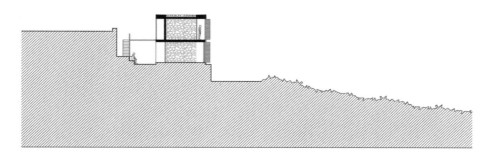

section

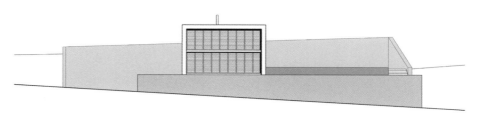

front elevation

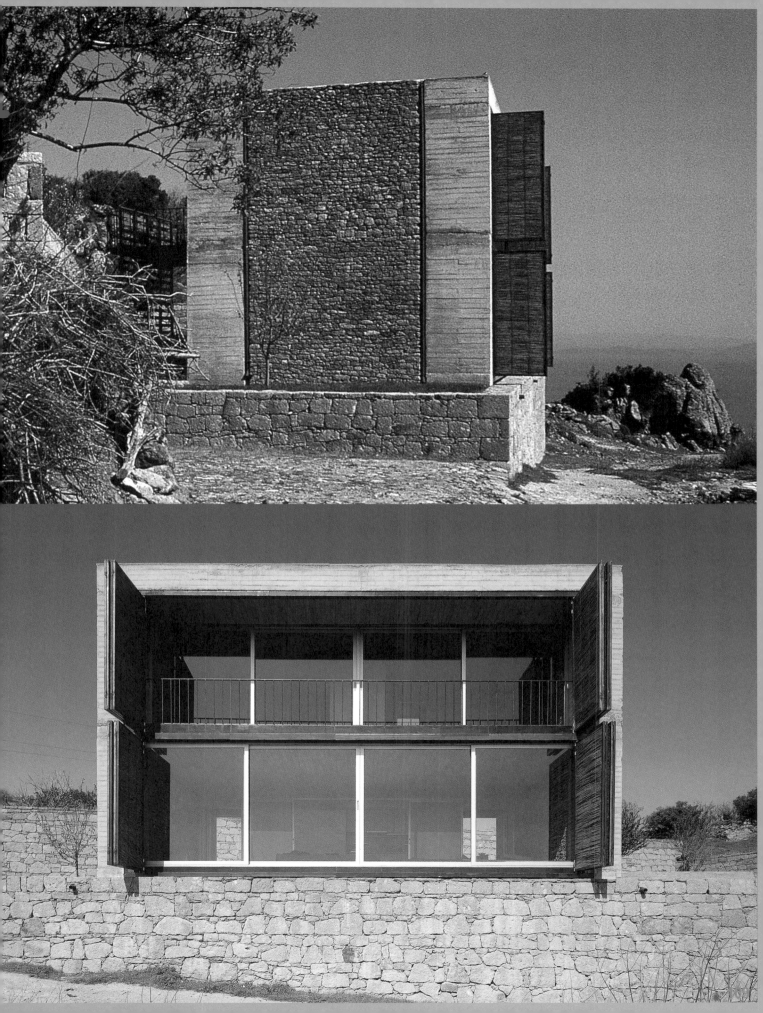

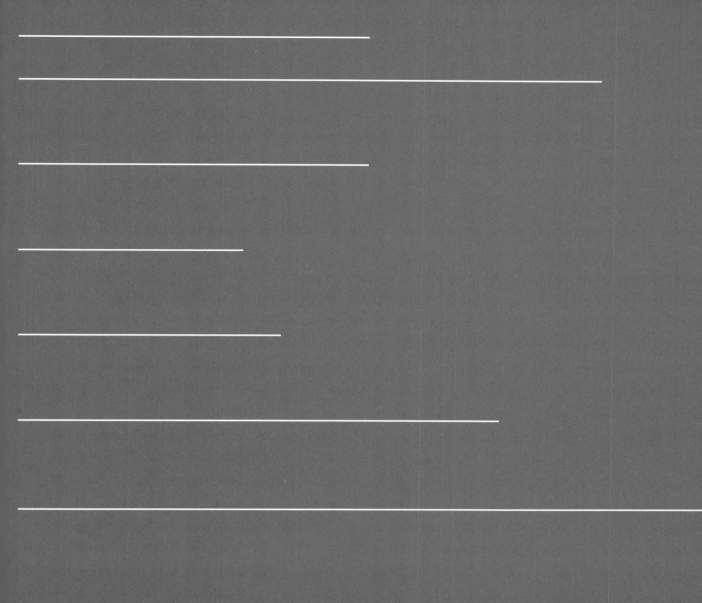

Kuala Lumpur, Malaysia

Petronas Towers

The Petronas Towers are the centrepiece of the mixed-use Kuala Lumpur City Centre complex, set in the heart of the commercial district of the city. Rising 452 metres, the towers were certified the world's tallest buildings by the Council of Tall Buildings and Urban Habitat in 1996. They are connected by a sky bridge at the forty-first and forty-second floors to facilitate inter-tower communication and circulation, while a multi-storey shopping and entertainment galleria connects the office towers at their bases. The complex also includes the Petroleum Discovery Centre, an art gallery, an 865-seat concert hall and a multimedia conference centre. The complex is at the forefront of technology, with intelligent systems controlling everything from telecommunications to fire safety. But at the same time, the buildings respond sensitively to their setting, with a form derived from an Islamic pattern, and extensive use of local materials.

The towers have become a popular example of contemporary architecture in Malaysia. Their elegant form makes them the country's most significant urban landmark – a dominant feature on the skyline of Kuala Lumpur and a national symbol of modern Malaysia that affirms the country's position on the world map.

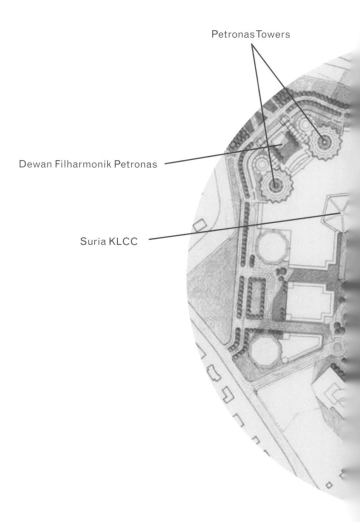

Petronas Towers

Dewan Filharmonik Petronas

Suria KLCC

This project has received an Award because it represents a new direction in skyscraper design, featuring advanced technology while symbolizing local and national aspirations. The project embodies several innovations, ranging from the use of unusually high-strength concrete to facilitate a soft-tube structural system, to an inventive vertical transportation concept and the integration of cutting-edge energy conservation systems. The success of this project lies in the manner in which it incorporates these technological innovations while generating a slender form that responds poetically to the broader landscape. The simple geometrical pattern that generates the plan not only uses space efficiently to maximize exposure to natural light, but also creates a rich spatial expression. The building has become an icon that expresses the sophistication of contemporary Malaysian society and builds on the country's rich traditions to shape a world city.

KLCC Park

For the last few decades Kuala Lumpur has been growing at a tremendous rate and has undergone many changes. In early 1981 the Malaysian Government decided to move the Selangor Turf Club and horse-racing track from the heart of the city to the periphery and to redevelop the site to meet the demands of urban and economic growth. The site occupies 40 hectares of land in the city's newly emerging business district – the 'Golden Triangle'. The economic boom years of the late 1970s and 1980s made this area very attractive for developers and speculators, and saw a proliferation of high-rise commercial buildings in a variety of styles and materials, built in an ad hoc manner with no central master plan. The decision to develop the racecourse site as a mixed-use complex, the Kuala Lumpur City Centre (KLCC), offered an opportunity to create an urban centre with a strong and distinctive identity ● and to reinforce Kuala Lumpur's emerging status as an international city in the twenty-first century. The KLCC was also intended to be a national symbol, reflecting the country's natural beauty and tropical greenery, as well its vibrant and rich cultural heritage.

An international competition to select a master plan for the new KLCC was organized in 1990. The concept of the winning plan by US firm Klages, Carter, Vail & Partners was an integrated mixed-use development – a city within a city – where people could work, live, shop and visit. In 1991 a second international competition was held for the design of the office tower complex and was won by Cesar Pelli & Associates. Work started on site in 1993, and the towers were opened in 1997. The official inauguration of the complex took place in 1999.

The project design was inspired by the minarets, stalactites and dome forms that are found in Kuala Lumpur's heterogeneous architecture, expressing the multicultural nature of Malaysian society. It is based on the concept of two interlocking squares that form an eight-pointed star – a traditional Islamic motif. This was modified by placing eight semicircles in the angles of the corners to create more floor space, so that the final floor plan has eight protruding points and eight lobes. ● Each tower rises eighty-eight storeys and provides 218,000 square metres of floor space, including an additional circular 'bustle' or annexe forty-four storeys high. The towers taper at six intervals, with the walls of the upper levels sloping inwards. Both towers are topped by a conical spire and a 73.5-metre-high pinnacle, giving the buildings an elegant and distinctive silhouette.

The structure supporting each of the towers comprises a ring of sixteen cylindrical columns of high-strength reinforced concrete, ● placed on the inner corners of the star-shaped plan to form a 'soft tube', with the columns linked by arched ring beams, also made of structural concrete. The columns are nearly 2.4 metres in diameter at the base of the building, but taper as they rise through the floors, as well as sloping towards the centre of the towers, enhancing the building's svelte profile. At the centre of each tower is a square core, which contains elevators, mechanical shafts and other services, with beams extending out to the perimeter columns. The use of high-strength concrete meant that core and column elements could be of economical size, increasing rentable space. The core measures approximately 23 by 23 metres and occupies 23 per cent of the floor plan – a relatively low ratio in comparison to other skyscrapers. Concrete construction also requires relatively simple equipment and is appropriate to the skills of the local workforce, and concrete aids wind resistance because of its inherent stiffness and damping properties.

Excavations at the early stages of construction revealed that the bedrock beneath the towers sloped steeply and was not strong enough to bear the weight of the buildings. Consequently, it was decided to move the towers about 60 metres to the south-east, where the buildings would sit on a concrete mat anchored to soil, not bedrock, by concrete friction piles. The foundation system of the towers consists of a 4.5-metre-thick piled raft supported on friction piles varying in depth from 40 metres to 105 metres.

The towers are connected at the forty-first and forty-second levels, 170 metres above street level, by a sky bridge, ● enabling inter-communication between the towers. The interchange also acts as a focal point for shared facilities such as the surau (prayer room) and executive dining rooms. The structural design of the sky bridge is complex because it has to accommodate differing movements from each tower. The solution is an inverted V-shaped two-hinged arch that supports the bridge in the centre, the struts ending in spherical bearings that can accommodate all movement. The resulting shape defines a symbolic gateway into the new city centre.

The towers are also joined at their base ● and in this shared area can be found an entrance lobby, featuring a variety of Malaysian motifs and materials integrated into a modern design. Also set between the towers is the Dewan Filharmonik Petronas, housing the Malaysian Philharmonic Orchestra. The concert hall ● combines flexible and up-to-date systems for acoustics and set arrangement with an intensively crafted and intricate space that brings together modern and traditional materials.

Also at the foot of the towers is a six-level, crescent-shaped retail and entertainment complex, ● Suria KLCC. In Malay 'suria' means sun, and here the sun is represented symbolically in the design of a cupola in the central atrium, which draws natural light into the complex while also providing ventilation. From the atrium, two 'streets', lined with over 300 shops, cafés and restaurants, extend along opposite axes. These streets are naturally lit by a linear skylight and lead to circular hubs at each end of the mall. In addition, the complex includes an art gallery, a specialized library and an interactive science discovery centre, as well as a four-storey underground car park for 5,400 cars.

At ground level the exterior façades feature arcades and canopies, evoking the 'five-foot way' of shophouses – the most ubiquitous building type in Malaysian cities. Shophouses are generally two storeys high, combining retail space on the lower floor and living space above, with a veranda on the ground floor at least 5 feet (1.5 metres) wide, creating covered routes to shelter pedestrians from the tropical sun and rain, while also providing a space for shopkeepers to display their wares. On the towers themselves, a curtain-wall system comprising a total of 33,000 panels is punctuated by stainless steel 'bullnose' and 'teardrop' sunscreen brackets that join together to give the appearance of a continuous silver ribbon around the building. ● The use of tinted laminated glass helps to reduce heat gain from the sunlight as well as ultraviolet transmission. As well as cutting the heat and glare entering the building, these walls reflect the play of light and shadow, expressing the lush tropical environment.

Throughout the complex, advanced communication systems and automatic controls reduce energy consumption and promote ease of use. One such system controls vertical transportation, which is provided by double-deck lifts ● capable of carrying twenty-six people per deck. These make better use of the core space and require less room for hoisting, increasing the efficiency of passenger transportation. The integrated energy-conservation concept of the towers is based on an innovative 'cool-recovery' system, which uses heat from exhaust air to power the cooling of outside air as it enters the building. The system reduces the amount of energy required to air condition the building by 50 per cent. Other high-technology intelligent systems manage building control, building security, telecommunications, fire alarms and the safety plan.

The Petronas Towers complex is very actively used. The columnless, open-plan offices in the towers provide flexible, state-of-the-art facilities for businesses, while the public areas have given the area a centre with a sense of place. Many visitors come to the complex simply because it is an attractive spot, and it has become the most highly frequented and fashionable visiting place in Kuala Lumpur. The complex combines modern technology with a sense of cultural identity and a sensitive responsiveness to its setting to create a powerful icon that symbolizes the country's progress. It has also introduced new architectural standards to Malaysia in terms of design, construction and technology. Most of all, the Petronas Towers embody an innovative and creative balance between modern global technology and local culture, making an important statement for the people of the region.

**Petronas Towers
Kuala Lumpur City Centre, Malaysia**

Client
Kuala Lumpur City Centre Holdings Sdn Bhd.

Architect
Cesar Pelli & Associates, US: Cesar Pelli, Design Principal; Fred Clarke, Collaborating Design Principal; Jon Pickard, Design Team Leader; Larry Ng, Project Manager; KLCC Behrard Architectural Division, Malaysia, architects of record; Adamson Associates, Canda, associate architects; Balmori Associates, US, and NR Associates, Malaysia, landscape design.

Engineers
Thornton-Tomasetti Engineers, US, and Ranhill Bersekutu Sdn Bhd, Malaysia, structural engineers; Flack + Kurtz, US, and KTA Tenaga Sdn Bhd, Malaysia, MEP engineers.

Consultants
STUDIOS, US, interior design; Walker Group, CNI, US, retail; Howard Brandston & Partners, US, lighting; Israel Berger & Associates, US, curtain wall; Shen, Milsom & Wilke, Inc, US acoustics; Katz Drago Company, Inc, Canada, vertical transportation; Lerch Bates & Associates, US, exterior maintenance; Techcord Consulting Group, Canda, security; Emery Vincent, Australia, graphics; Rolf Jensen & Associates, US, life safety; Wilbur Smith Associates, Singapore, traffic; Central Parking Systems, US, parking; Ove Arup and Partners, UK, and Arup Jururunding, Malaysia, site and civil engineering; Rowan Williams Davies and Irwin RWDI, Canada, wind-tunnel testing.

Contractors
Tower 1 – Mayjus Joint Venture: MMC Engineering & Construction Co. Ltd, Malaysia; Ho Hup Construction Sdn Bhd, Malaysia; Hazama Corporation, Malaysia; JA Jones Construction Co Ltd, US; Mitsubishi Corporation, Japan.
Tower 2 – SKJ Joint Venture: Samsung Engineering & Construction Co Ltd, North Korea; Kuk Dong Engineering & Construction Co Ltd, Malaysia; Syarikat Jasatera Sdn Bhd, Malaysia; Dragages and Bachy-Soletanche, Singapore; First Nationwide Engineering Sdn Bhd, Malaysia.

Commission	December 1991
Design	January 1992–June 1994
Construction	April 1993–August 1999
Occupation	January 1997–August 1999
Site area, KLCC	40.5 hectares
Site area, Petronas and retail	5.8 hectares
Built area	218,000m² each tower 994,000m² total Petronas complex
Cost	US$800,000,000

Established in 1977, Cesar Pelli & Associates is an architectural practice based in New Haven, Connecticut, US. The firm has worked with corporate, government and private clients to design major public spaces, museums, airports, laboratories, performing arts centres, academic buildings, hotels, office and residential towers and mixed-use projects. The Design Principal, Cesar Pelli (b. 1926, Argentina), served as Dean of the School of Architecture at Yale University from 1977 to 1984, where he continues to lecture. Mr Pelli has written extensively on architectural issues and his work is widely published and exhibited, with seven books and several issues of professional journals dedicated to his designs and theories. He has received ten honorary degrees, over a hundred awards for design excellence and is a Fellow of the American Institute of Architects, and a member of the American Academy of Arts and Letters, the National Academy of Design, the International Academy of Architecture, and the Academie d'Architecture de France. Mr Pelli was awarded the American Institute of Architects (AIA) Gold Medal in 1995 in recognition of his lifetime achievements and outstanding contributions.

Websites
Cesar Pelli & Associates
www.cesar-pelli.com
Kuala Lumpur City Centre
www.klcc.com.my

west elevation

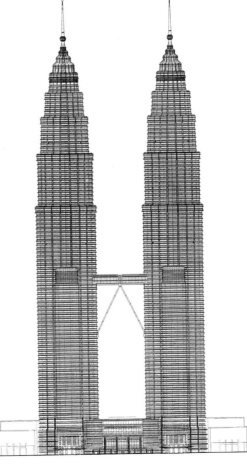

north elevation

east elevation

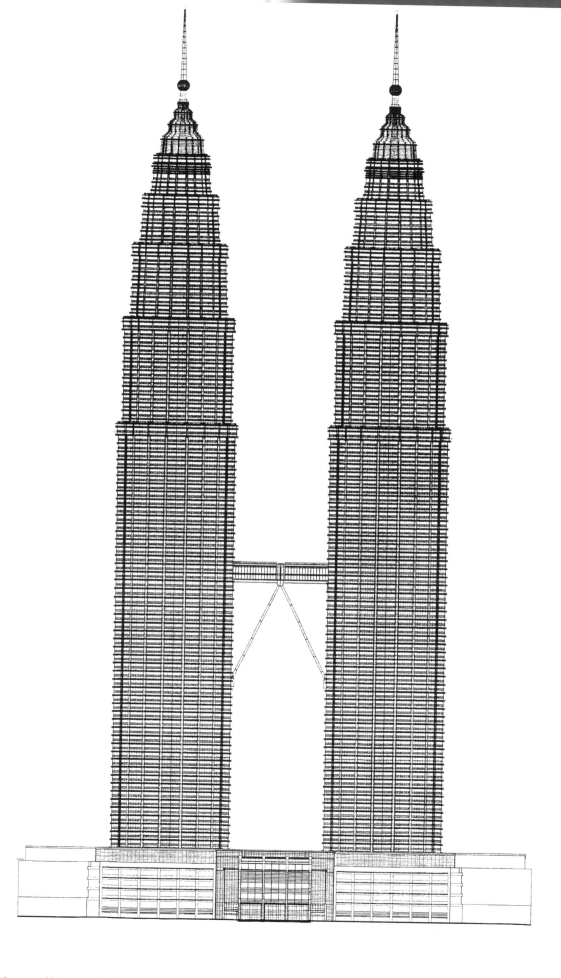

south elevation

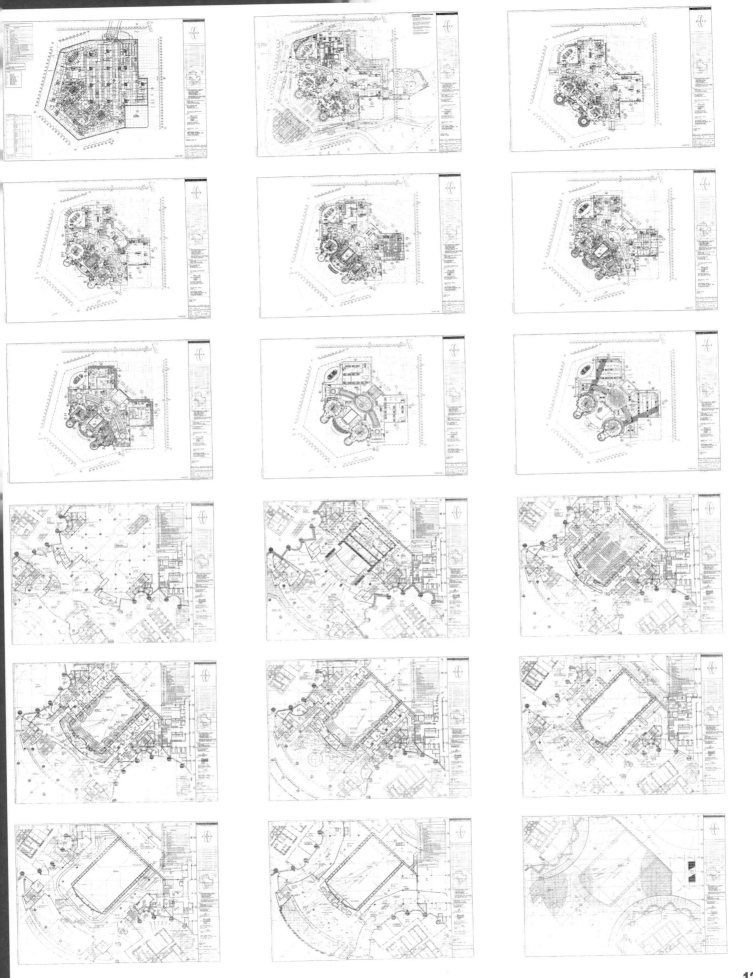

Petronas Towers – Kuala Lumpur, Malaysia • Architecture and Polyphony

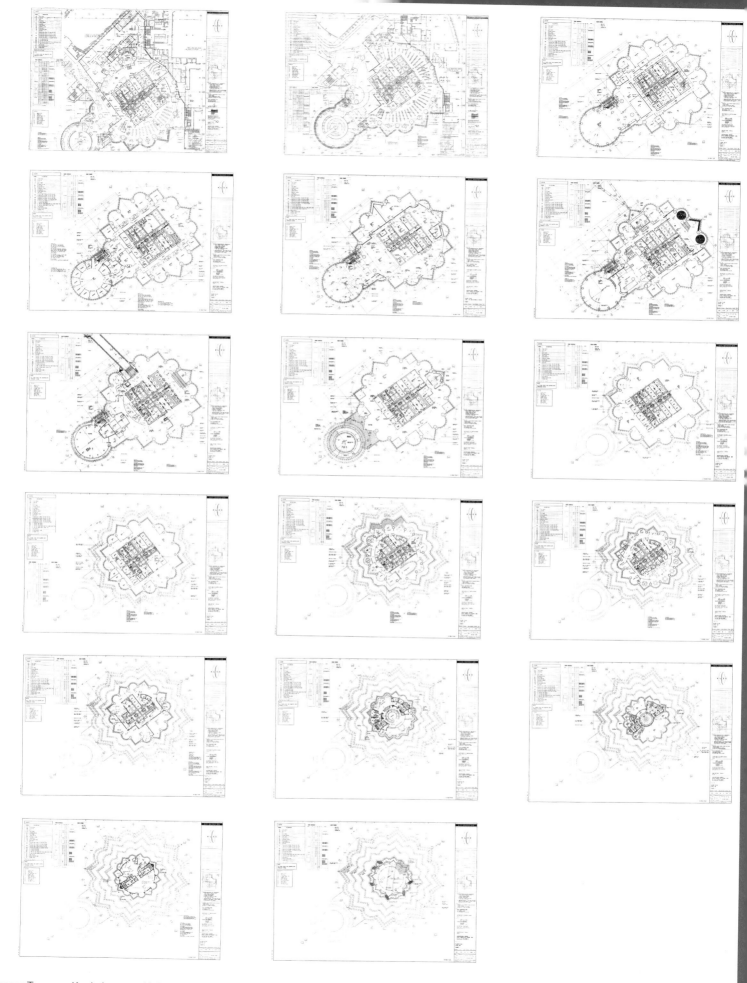

2004 Award Steering Committee and Master Jury
Seated, left to right: Reinhard Schulze, Ghada Amer, Elías Torres Tur, Billie Tsien, Prince Hussain Aga Khan,
His Highness the Aga Khan, Farshid Moussavi, Hanif Kara, Jafar Tukan, Rahul Mehrotra, Modjtaba Sadria.
Standing, left to right: Suha Özkan, Jacques Herzog, Charles Correa, Babar Khan Mumtaz, Mohsen Mostafavi,
Akram Abu Hamdan, Glenn Lowry, Abdou Filali-Ansary, Farrokh Derakhshani.

The Grammar of Architecture
Reinhard Schulze

Architecture is art in form, or form in art, or the art of forming, or the performing of art in form. Being art, architecture deals with aesthetic meaning in specific form.

Architecture is culture. As culture, architecture is part of a semiotic repertoire that gives meaning to the world and to the materials used in building. In a way, architecture makes culture of the material world: a stone takes on meaning when it is enclosed in a wall, as does concrete – the result of a chemical procedure – when it is moulded into significant form. In other words, architecture deals with the material world in the same way that human beings use linguistic signs such as sounds and words to produce a phrase by which they interpret the world around them.

But parallels between language and architecture are limited. On the one hand, both employ a set of conventions that are used in expressions. Language, however, is not free in assembling its repertoire of signs: it has to observe grammar, which renders expressions comprehensible. Human beings are not the sovereigns of grammar; they are subject to grammar, which is historical or, as some believe, an innate mental concept.

Though architecture is subject to conventions in the sense that it relies upon materials that are accepted as part of the building process – stone, brick, concrete, glass, wood, component parts, and so on – it does not employ a fixed grammar. Over the course of history, however, building schemes have been affected by traditions or conventions, which may be considered a substitute for grammar. As a result, we might come across building traditions that are called 'Chinese' or 'Muslim' or 'Christian'. These traditions are defined not only in buildings that represent the specific meaning of a given culture (a mosque, a temple or a church), but also in buildings whose inhabitants or architects were attached to those cultures in the broadest, most general way.

Architecture has always relied upon the knowledge of specialists and professionals who have learned the art of building; it has never become a mental concept whereby people build according to a cultural tradition that is 'innate'. Consequently, 'Islamic architecture', for example, is not a concept per se: it derives from those professionals who have constantly reinvented building traditions as Islamic. The same, of course, is true for all other cultural traditions.

As language, architecture is a means of interpretation that is based on universals and specifics. The sound 'b', for example, is universal – there is hardly any language in the world that does not contain the sound 'b'. Perhaps some people will articulate 'b' in a phonetically different way, but anyone will be able to recognize when a speaker is producing a word by using the phoneme 'b'. There are, of course, sounds specific to certain languages: the Arabic phoneme 'dad' served as a characterization of Arabic speakers as 'speakers of the dad'. In general, however, specifics derive from the arrangement of the sounds typical of certain languages and from the grammar that arranges words as syntagmata. In architecture, there are also universals: materials, functions (such as shelter) and even forms (if a building is to give shelter, then it must be closed and have a roof). But the specifics are much more visible. As we are accustomed to accepting these universals as standard, our eyes focus on the specific forms: the arrangement of the materials, the proportions, the style, and so on.

As already noted, architecture and language both serve as a means of interpretation. This interpretation may relate to the world in which a building is located, or it may relate to the material used. If an architect wants to give meaning to a certain material and employs it in an original way, then we may say that architecture becomes art. The building itself may be an expression of the architect's ambition to deal with the material and, at the same time, an interpretation of a specific meaning that is not dependent on the material used.

When we look at a building, we may ask about its 'artistic' expression or meaning. If we accept the analogy between language and architecture, then every building may be read or understood as a phrase or a paragraph or even as a whole book, with building schemes based on a given architectural grammar. To read architecture means to reconstruct the (hidden?) meaning that informed the building.

But it is difficult to read the meaning if a building is based on a grammar and a vocabulary that have first to be learned. In the modern age, however, cultural specifics have become paradigmatic for globally accepted universals. In my view, this is the most striking effect of modernity: today, buildings based on a local vernacular do not necessarily express culturally different meanings but clothe universals in tradition.

'Islamic architecture' is architectural modernity using cultural repertoires that are conventionally associated with Islamic traditions. After most Islamic traditions merged with modernity during the course of the nineteenth century, anyone composing large architectural forms in the Muslim world followed the history of modernity. But, being part of modernity, architecture in the Muslim world accepted the disassociation of Islamic traditions from general building patterns. Consequently, we have two diverging processes. First, Islam has become a concept that intentionally gives meaning to a building – that is, a building becomes 'Islamic'. For this, Islam has to be defined on an architectural level. What are the attributes required to make a global public recognize a building as Islamic? This concept of an 'Islamic grammar' of architecture is modern; it differs strongly from the architectural concepts used in building a mosque in a Muslim environment in pre-modern times. Second, buildings use attributes of modernity without referring to an Islamic repertoire. A family home in Abu Dhabi, for example, can hardly be read in terms of a specific cultural tradition. If architects want a building to be associated with a specific cultural environment, they simply include some cultural 'marks', mostly derived from Orientalism. These accessories do not change the modern identity of a building at all.

There is a third alternative process. Modernity has tended to re-evaluate and reify tradition. Architecture is susceptible to reification. Modernity has incorporated traditions as ethnic repertoires that it seeks to ascribe to various peoples. Orientalism is only one example of several discursive procedures that have sought to embody and revive specific ethnic values in architectural form. It has often been stated that this process is important in order to accommodate modern architectural ambitions within local conditions. It should be observed, however, that most of these local conditions are not a historical continuation of pre-modern traditions but inventions of the last 200 years.

Traditionally architecture is conservative and relies mostly on experience and positive examples. In the Middle Ages, for instance, the memory of architects was much more important than written or drawn representations of buildings, because a new building could be considered as a repetition of an earlier successful one. But since no building site is like any other, any new building had to accommodate different conditions and featured slight changes that made it specific. If a third building was built, the master builder then had available two examples to serve as a model. He had to decide which model to use, and in turn adapt his own building to local conditions. Thus, he had to select, copy and accommodate – in other words, to change the initial model.

But, since the eighteenth century, this evolutionary process has been replaced by the creation of abstract styles spliced to traditions. With the establishment after the 1850s of art as a concept through which to criticize tradition, architects began to invent new traditions. Typically, they were not able to rely upon memory, but had to create written (drawn) schemes of building prototypes, which might have been based on their reading of classical buildings such as temples, and so on. By the incorporation of art into architecture, architecture was transformed into a profession and a 'free' art of building. Freed from tradition, architecture started to define its own cultural code – one that played with invented traditions and modern inventions. Thus, modernity has created a new global vocabulary of architecture that includes various interpretations of vernaculars.

This process had already begun in the eighteenth century. Ottoman master builders of the Tulip Period (1718–30) accepted European Baroque styles as global vocabularies and incorporated selected 'Islamic' traditions into this global pattern to render a building 'Islamic'. The process reached its first peak in the second half of the nineteenth century, when not only architectural details but also building types, structures and organizational frameworks were globalized.

Architecture in the Muslim world of today is part of a global history of modernity. It shares the challenges and experiences and the strengths and weaknesses of modernity. Some parts of the Muslim world show a greater affinity with European modernity; others are closer to US modernity. But notwithstanding this internal pluralism, the global history of modern architecture is an integral part of the Muslim world's architectural history.

Ten Thoughts During Ten Days
as a Jury Member
Billie Tsien

1. As the only American on the Award Master Jury during the reign of George W. Bush, I felt apprehensive as I flew to Geneva for the first meetings during January 2004. I was worried that I was a representative of a policy and a regime with which I deeply disagreed. My primary reason for coming was to try to gain greater knowledge of Muslim cultures, which are usually presented as monolithic.

2. The discussions were illuminating, frustrating, inspiring and hilarious – sometimes simultaneously. We were architects, artists, philosophers and sociologists and we each took turns wearing the others' hats.

8. Surprisin

3. The Award carries with it the criterion of social responsibility, which is one that does not generally apply to architecture awards. I felt like a patient sitting in the chair at an optometrist's office. A large apparatus is lowered in front of my face as I stare ahead at letters and different sets of lenses are placed in front of my eyes. Which set is better – the first or the second? Which lens is the controlling one? There was a new lens set in front of my judgemental eyes. How do I see clearly with this new lens in place?

4. In Geneva everything closes down at 7.00pm.

5. The primary school in Burkina Faso was a very important project for me. It was a project that looked wonderful with all sets of lenses dropped in front of my eyes. Difficult circumstances gave birth to invention. The bent bars used in place of conventional steel or wood let the roof levitate above the building like a giant wing. It is a school built by villagers from a design by an architect who is the son of the village chief. It is a building of beauty and economy. It is unlikely that I would ever have seen this project (or indeed most of the others) if I had not been part the Jury and for this, and much more, I am grateful to the Aga Khan Award for Architecture.

6. We struggled because there were two issues that we wanted to highlight through the Award process. We hope that future submissions will produce architecture of excellence that reflects these issues. Firstly, public infrastructure; and secondly, projects that address the position of women, either through their programme briefs or through the recognition of women as architects and clients.

7. A visit to the house that Le Corbusier designed for his mother in Vevey confirmed the ability of an ecstatic yet sensible simplicity to amaze, inspire and bring joy.

ossible to smoke cigars at the dinner table in restaurants in Switzerland.

9. I feel proud of our process and of our choice of projects. Each one stands on its own as a significant piece of architecture or restoration. Each one has recognized and directly addressed a need or illustrated a principle.

10. My sense of the world has changed. I leave this experience as a member of the Jury with optimism and hope. To build is always work. To try to make a building into architecture is a struggle. To choose to engage in this struggle is an act of affirmation and optimism. It implies a belief in a shared future and a belief that the future can be made better. What better focus can there be for our lives here together on earth?

Cults of Collaboration
Hanif Kara

The projects selected in this cycle of the Aga Khan Award for Architecture show perfectly the very best that building projects across the Islamic world can offer in terms of aesthetics, skill, teamwork and creativity. What is more, most of these projects have responded to their sites, to differing scales and to issues like sustainability in a wholly admirable way, while maintaining design excellence.

But there is a problem. By choosing exemplary projects, any award system also shines a light on the many more schemes in both the Islamic and wider world where such standards are falling short. We need to ask why and to ponder what the engineering profession that I belong to can offer to the mix in a bid to raise quality across the board.

Both of these points – the reasons for failure and the quest for solutions – arise because engineering today, viewed at least from one perspective, is at a crossroads on a number of issues. The first of these concerns the importance of design, which I believe is being eroded, primarily because of the way society has gone through sudden irreversible changes. As societies undergo rapid change – and the Industrial Revolution is a good example of this – there is a tendency for them to 'professionalize'. The massive, rapid advances made in materials over the twenty-five years that the Award has been running are another example, with an estimate of a staggering 60,000 different kinds of materials now available. But during that Industrial Revolutionary spurt, within industry in the Western world, architecture and engineering both found themselves veering into an 'over-professionalized' mode, with the result that a greater faith was placed in technology. What fell by the wayside during this process was a craft-based approach to design – there was a drift away from the 'makers', and professionalism became the more important issue.

It is true that the rise of computer and information technology today has ushered in something of a new mini-wave of this craft-based approach, but less design work is being done, and constructors the world over are doing too much of the work and too many of the drawings on behalf of architects and engineers. It is this erosion, particularly of the main currency of design – the skill of drawing – that sets a very dangerous precedent, both for the professions it will affect and for the wider world as a whole, because buildings will be of a lesser quality.

So, who in the process chain is best placed to try and ameliorate this problem, through knowledge about the ways that materials will perform, for example? Who can act as the bridge between somebody dreaming about a scheme and somebody making it? I believe that this role can be fulfilled by the engineer, who, like all bridges, can be used in both directions to provide entry ways and passages.

The second specific area faced at that crossroads by the field of engineering concerns the essence of the relationship between engineers and architects. This too is facing erosion because, as architects do less drawing work and do not talk enough to engineers, schemes of dubious quality will emerge. The engineer is facing a number of growing gaps – such as that between the developed and underdeveloped worlds – that have come about as a result of globalization. For me, at one level, it is a myth that globalization offers endless choice and opportunity: the construction industry seems to be dominated by a few large contractors who form alliances with materials groups. This reduces client choice and does nothing to progress architecture of note. If the materials or system of building are predetermined or too influenced by relationships, then the building will suffer. The engineer, with his or her understanding of materials and the construction process, is well placed to stand up to this danger.

If we get it right and make sure that we are all pluralistic, shunning the cult of the individual but embracing a cult of change, then this century should see a renaissance in the way we produce buildings. But along the way some other things need to change. The engineer needs an improved image and should be closer to the public at large – often he or she is seen simply as the one unimaginatively making architects' designs stand up, or as the scientist building the tallest or biggest structure. Mostly this problem has stemmed from the profession's seeming inability to project a good image of itself, and its resistance to a radical over-haul of institutions of architecture and engineering inherited from previous eras. Education can come to the rescue here. The Aga Khan Award is making progress on the educational front by disseminating information about design across the globe. But in the past there have been leaders such as the Swiss engineer Heinz Isler, who sold his own particular agenda on self-supporting shells all around the world. Less and less of this inspirational teaching is happening, partly again, in my view, because of the downsides of globalization, where most things can be downloaded from the Internet.

In the end, then, a better sense of collaboration and team-work is the key to finding success in the buildings we create, and it is a principle that has a notable advocate from history. Frank Lloyd Wright, the master designer, gave priority to engineering. As an engineer as well as an architect (he left engineering school three months short of his degree), Wright saw no essential conflict between engineering and design. In fact, he believed the opposite: that new aesthetics are the inescapable consequence of new engineering techniques.

The engineer – with a few exceptions – operates in a supportive role for the architect. But the two roles need to be blurred enough so that when they combine – one might call it 'engitecture' – a better product is the result, and both disciplines together forge a new path, which is necessary for the survival and prosperity of both architecture and engineering. The projects premiated in this cycle of the Aga Khan Award are a testament that this is already happening – but also that it is not happening quite enough.

It is not all doom and gloom, however. I have touched already on how the use of information technology is giving rise to a new wave of craft culture and mass-customization. The advancement of information technology as the primary tool for urbanists, architects and engineers is opening a new and more intimate relationship between them. Architecture now has more science to it, while engineering has more art to it. In the field of architecture, engineering design is happily becoming an intrinsic part of a new generation of form and organization. Architects will now design using an image of a simulated stress pattern, for example; as little as three decades ago, they would not have even seen such an image. Similarly, in the past an architect would not know why an engineer said something would not work – today he or she has access to that information. The relationship between architects and designers is now transparent because the types of barrier that used to exist between the two have been broken down. Furthermore, an architect does not now need to tell the engineer why he or she is choosing a certain orientation or aesthetic for a building because the engineer is beginning to understand more and more about what archi-tects do. Each profession questions the other more, and collaborates better by doing so.

So, on one level it should be easy for engineers and archi-tects to become closer, for the good of every project. This is the ideal relationship – where the naturally divergent thoughts of the architect are married to the convergent ones of the engineer, and each discipline begins to use and learn elements of the other, to the advantage of both. This collab-oration is already becoming the ethic of new designers.

'Three conditions architecture must accomplish:
Utilitas (utility), *Firmitas* (durability, permanence,
resistance) and *Venustas* (beauty).'

Marcus Vitruvius Pollio (fl. 46-30 BC), *De Architectura*, book 1, chapter 3, section 2

'Don't underestimate the power
of ugliness, for it is the doorway
to stupidity, which, in turn, is the
doorway to evil…Everything tends
to begin with aesthetics; hence,
ugliness appears first, followed
by stupidity.'

Rafael Sánchez Ferlosio, 'La forja de un plumífero',
Archipiélago 31, 1997

Man conceives architecture as a permanent protecting veil
against his own frailness and transience, a means to survive
with dignity in his natural habitat. Architecture provides a
way of being in the world and helps us build universal values,
both spiritual and symbolic. Therefore, it contains an ethical
commitment that should be conveyed by aesthetics.

Each work of architecture is the result of an experimental
process of acquaintance with and transformation of our
environment by means of a specific response to particular
and existing social needs. An architect must build and design
with responsibility, generosity, a sense of justice and balance
(avoiding the unnecessary); with flexibility and independence,
taking chances and challenging the unknown and with the
desire to change and improve.

An architect must have the sensibility necessary to understand places and their cultures, to interpret the different
options he encounters and to be familiar with the disciplines
of architecture. He must strive for inspiration to achieve
those indispensable and unforeseeable moments of emotion,
of light and understanding. And he should always apply
a slight bit of irony so as never to take himself too seriously,
and be able to wink at the tragic side of life.

A Swiss retreat
Many hours in front of Lac Léman and Mont Blanc. Many hours
sitting, listening to ourselves and to each other. (If we spoke
it was by turns, raising a finger to request permission from
the president, although sometimes, someone – too often me
– could not hold back and outrageously broke the established
order to say something.) We looked like a class where everyone was a pupil and a professor at the same time. After ten
days non-stop (with the exception of an unexpected trip to
Le Corbusier's mama's little house) of necessary conflicts to
reach a final agreement, of help from the outstanding staff of
the Aga Khan Award for Architecture, of making new friends,
of learning and trying to have a good time, I found I had
gained 2.5 kilograms when I returned to Barcelona (the
Geneva hotel's scales were elegantly out of order).

'Architecture: The art of designing and building buildings.'

Royal Academy Dictionary of the Spanish Language

'The first function of art is to surprise, to break the habits of perception and to make the old new.'

Cesar Aira, quoted by Enrique Vila-Matas, *El Pais*, 28 June 2003

On Bibliotheca Alexandrina●
A library stocks treasures of thought in every possible form for the enjoyment of citizens, experts, students or idle visitors. Its presence in a city must be felt: one must filter the other, from inside space to outside space (and vice versa). <u>A library is a source of intellectual exchange</u> (not compulsory but unavoidable). It is a symbolic temple of memory, or a room where we can recognize and find the stuff of which our memory is made. (It is essential to have a good fire protection system.)

On Gando Primary School●
<u>Education, knowledge, is the seed of independence and liberty, of civilization</u>. It is the weapon with which power can be challenged – a weapon for respect, coexistence, for understanding the world and feeling solidarity with each other. A school is the temple, the house where we identify collective knowledge, the permanent and the new. A school is where we become aware of our individuality within some-thing universal. A school is also a teacher and some pupils, anywhere, in any space. But teaching and learning will be enhanced by this space's dignity. Good architecture will be one more lesson.

On Sandbag Shelter Prototypes●
Research can be undertaken to take the edge off poverty, misery and neglect, to help people survive, and to counter-act natural and human disasters provoked by ambition, disdain, power and fanaticism, among other epidemics. <u>Many grains of sand can help build resistance against the unfair or the unexpected – a way of doing justice. A prototype can be the seed of a universal solution</u>, and the more it is inexpensive – as all significant research should be – the more it will be welcome.

On the Restoration of Al-Abbas Mosque●
Women and men in every culture have always fought to improve their image, their presence, to look younger, to please others with facelifts, make-up, prostheses, slimming, clothes, hairdressers. Old age is now regarded as a state of decrepitude, neglect and marginalization, when instead we should accept the presence of our elders and their memories, their experience, their wisdom, as a living bridge to our past and our origins. Without them we cannot know our childhood. We are all contemporary. Their conditions of living and health must be improved (and we, in turn, will improve), not with unnecessary body-lifts and make-up that turns them into caricatures (cockatoos) or rejuvenated mummies, but with appropriate dress, corrected teeth, hearing aids, pacemakers, heating and cooling systems at home, protection and social care. This is the responsibility of everyone, every society and every institution. <u>If life is to retain its meaning, the old and the new must coexist and exchange their customs and their knowledge</u>.

On B2 House●
A house is both a stage of individuality and the door to a community. It is also a social right. The history of architecture can be understood through individual houses. In them there is always something experimental, hedonistic (sometimes nouveau riche, at other times modest), provocative, pastiche-like, ridiculous; and, most of the time, discreet, anodyne or imitative. In formal proposals for isolated houses, which are often small and do not have demanding programmes, there is a constant exchange of ideas with the other visual arts. <u>If an architect can design a house, he or she will be able success-fully to design a hospital, a school, an auditorium, a factory or a swimming pool – which are all different types of houses or shelters</u>.

On Petronas Towers●
Skyscrapers are not indispensable. If they do not turn the surrounding city into a desert, there is nothing wrong with them. (In midtown Manhattan, the quality of the streets and public spaces is independent of the height of the buildings.) A large group of skyscrapers can attain a magical character, while an isolated one, unprotected, is much more hazardous. <u>Just like any other singular building, the skyscraper should be thoroughly justified before it is built because its presence will inevitably be overwhelming. Therefore, its architecture must be excellent</u>. Skyscrapers are symbols, like minarets or belfries; they are trademarks of corporations (and their profitability); sometimes they are fanciful bibelots. What a craze to build the highest building! It's like the 100-metre race. It can be done, of course, but it will always be topped by a lightning rod just to reach some clouds. Why not the longest buildings (horizonscrapers), or the shortest (landscrapers)?

We are narrators
of sweet and happy tales
Tales of the
dense bush
With a mountain behind
a spring in front
Tales of
the warm hands of a friend
in cold nights of the city.

Mehdi Akhavan Sales

Opening

Having studied attentively close to 400 projects submitted for this cycle of the Aga Khan Award, listening carefully to the evaluation criteria of architect members of the Master Jury, making a great effort to bear in mind what was presented to us as the accumulated experience of many cycles of the Award, I have not become opinionated about architecture and the internal debates concerning it. At most, I feel a bit less ignorant in this very rich field, and am experiencing greater sensitivity towards it in my daily life. My views, including those expressed here, remain those of a person on the edge, on the margin. This position of being on the margin – not geographically but epistemologically – remains very dear to me. If my understanding is correct, by including non-architects on the Master Jury, the Award's Steering Committee intended to enlarge the scope of arguments beyond the field of architecture in a narrow sense, in order to reach a more comprehensive view.

Meanwhile, the specificity of architecture as a field, intimately linked to our existence in this world, and the depth of the debates surrounding architecture, the accelerated speed of its changes, the growing impact it is having on our personal, social, cultural and aesthetic experiences, and its emergence – at least on the symbolic level – as one of the ingredients of contemporary global-ization, are giving architecture a greater capacity to influence, or at least to find an echo in, a broader social context. Put differently, as a field, architecture has its own 'gates' – important, specific and consciously maintained gates. But because of its capacity to resonate in the lives of non-architects, it has become paradoxical to build and maintain walls that delimit architecture from other fields in society. It seems to me important to recognize architecture as a field by acknowledging its gates, but also to scrutinize the field from its margins, allowing its appropriation by non-architects, conceptually as well as paradigmatically. Can we hope that architects will accept having wall-less gates, indicating the existence of a field but also inviting outside views into it?

Analogy

I feel that it is important to explain my use of the term 'field'. Conceptually, my critical understanding of 'field' starts with the work of the French sociologist Pierre Bourdieu (1930–2002). In *Homo Academicus* (1984) he became a systemic denunciator of social arrangements in the production of contemporary knowledge in the academic and professional worlds, by opening perspectives beyond the gates to out-siders. Please bear with me: I intend more to mention a trajectory than to provide a conceptual demonstration. With Bourdieu's concept of field, the guardians of the gates of the academic and professional fields became more visible. These guardians intend to define the exclusivity of their fields with the purpose of establishing personal power bases within academia and, through it, within society at large.

Portal near Le Croisic, western France

This first conceptual unveiling of the 'gate' was completed through semiotics, emanating from a different perspective and, interestingly enough, because of architectural monuments, another interpretation of 'gate' was offered. This interpretation has three monumental references. One is a secular portal in a remote area of western France, more precisely in the Loire Atlantique region, close to the village of Le Croisic. This gate is in the middle of nowhere, near a road, and it delimits nothing; it stands in a kind of no man's land and is, at best, a landmark.[1]

A *torii* gate, Japan

Another 'gate' without any apparent walls is the *torii* in Japanese Shinto shrines. The *torii* – a gate built with a wide variety of materials, shapes and colours – indicates the beginning of a sacred, divine space, which is inhabited by the god of the shrine. It indicates the symbolic border between two worlds. The power of the deity located beyond the *torii* is supposed to make itself felt in the profane world outside the shrine. Physical openness, here, represents the enclosure of the sacred ground. The *torii* gate without any wall is, in fact, the gate of a powerful invisible wall. Passing through the gate signifies an act of submission to the transcendental senses that the gate designates.[2,3]

Different designs of the *torii*

The third example is closer to my reading of the possibilities for interaction between architects and non-architects within the field of architecture. This is the story of a Buddhist temple on the outskirts of Ome, a city to the west of Tokyo. The name of the temple is Monshuin, derived from the school of Buddhism that is based on the principles of *mon* (listening to the teaching of Buddha, or, in my interpretation, knowing), *shi* (which can also be read as *omou*, understanding), and *shuu* (mastering, action or practice – again in a simplified interpretation). This temple, built between 1532 and 1555, is based on these principles and is intended to be a place for different people to meet, a place for people to experience the transcendental, and a place that allows those who enter to express themselves, to feel a sense of emancipation. From the time of its inception, the gate of the temple was designed and built not to have any walls. To my knowledge, it is unique in Japanese Buddhism.[4]

Gate of the Monshuin Temple, Ome, Japan

I have a concept of a 'gate' that indicates lines of demarcation but is also open to inclusion. From this perspective, I tried to clarify my own stance towards the deliberations of the Award Master Jury, prompting the following thoughts.

Place and time for living

If the central question of modernity – the quality of human presence in the world – is still valid, then architecture represents this inquiry in a multitude of ways, sometimes consciously. Universal as it is, this question takes on more specific meanings according to time and place. Here place is understood in both senses: in physical terms – places where living occurs; and as a space where subjectivities, tastes and consciousness meet. Time also refers to the contemporary – living in the twenty-first century – and to duration in time, the depth of historical awareness. In these terms, the profession that conceives places becomes responsible for acts of civilization.

Is it too much to claim that architecture is a reflection of the accumulation of ten thousand years of human knowledge and experience? Maybe not, if we consider the multitude of levels at which architects willingly intervene in the contemporary 'matrix of aesthetics' – a matrix that tries to deal with diversity, heterogeneity, even a certain hybridity, while at the same time retaining a certain harmony.

But the quality of our lives, which remains the fundamental aspect of our presence in the world, has become in part confused because of the quality of the spaces that we are building and inhabiting. This confusion and the problems it generates are such that we are forced to say we have become a society at risk. Does naming this confusion 'Post-modern' help to resolve this aspect of our human condition?

The need of the contemporary 'matrix of aesthetics' for a sense of beauty in our daily life is forcing the transcendental sense of space, manifested in the past in sacred places, to become part of our immanent life. Daily life requires ethics and invented spaces must establish, rejuvenate and reflect these ethics.

How can we maintain flexibility in the interaction of humans with nature and avoid alienation, while remaining open to innovative approaches in building private spaces and retaining a public sense of belonging in our shrunken but fragmented world? How can society's rising awareness of issues such as accessibility for the elderly, children and people with disabilities be a focal point in the design of buildings when economic disparities are creating urgent issues such as homelessness – an acute problem for large parts of the earth's population? Furthermore, how can this latter issue be resolved without giving rise to the dehumanizing social conditions of a modern quasi-ghetto? And all of these issues exist in a broader social context in which large-scale corruption, including corruption in the field of architecture, renders regulations rather cosmetic. Need we be reminded that schools in Turkey and hospitals in Iran, destroyed over the heads of children and patients during earthquakes, were mostly recent buildings designed by certified architects? One could add the partial collapse of Terminal 2E at Charles de Gaulle Airport in Paris as a more recent case. Rehabilitating an ethic of non-pretentiousness and of rigour, forming a mechanism of checks and balances, making it possible to create a beauty that is simple but can invoke complexity, and keeping in mind a sense of our presence in the world – these are our major challenges.

Expanding

My experience on the Master Jury has enlarged the above concerns. Arguing about some of them goes beyond the intentions of this essay, but I shall mention just a few.

Fragmenting

Can the practice of architecture at the beginning of the twenty-first century, through the contiguities that it establishes, consider itself above the social fragmentation that it is generating – a fragmentation that is making living together more difficult? Or does architecture consider itself not to be bound – to be free of any social identity? If this is the case, the only elements that count should be the materials used and the styles chosen.

Tool for a mirage

Another concern is modernization, which in my vocabulary is the opposite of modernity. Modernity is understood as the social acceptance that human beings have the faculty of questioning everything and anything. This faculty is the most emancipating factor for human beings individually as well as collectively. In contrast with modernity, modernization is an attempt by the state to substitute itself for society, and to impose a model of what it would like society to become – a model borrowed from a different society with another historicity. In the last sixty years, policies of modernization, coupled with all categories of development theory, have been the major cause of acculturation. Architecture, linked with urban planning (a link that unfortunately exists only rarely) and landscaping, has been very active in this process of cultural amputation, whereas all three have the means to become active engines for enculturation – for generating hybrid creativity and life-enhancing experiences.

Castrated myth

Myth, as a living factor, appropriated by social actors, could have powerful capacities. A castrated myth is one emptied of its vital, flexible and relevant character. Traditionalism, by extracting traditions from their historical context and transforming them into ideological references with which to discipline society, acts as a castrated myth. Traditionalism, as a fake replica, prevents the invention of traditions as the only ways that societies can negotiate being and living together. Here also, architecture and urban design have been instrumental.

Neophyte

I entered the Award Master Jury discussions with many doubts about the possibility of making any contribution. Those doubts remain intact. Meanwhile, the experience has sparked new enquiries; for example, how to integrate issues related to architecture, urbanism and landscape more actively into my own research and teaching practices. Concepts such as the public sphere, public space, intersubjectivity and empowerment have become much more relevant. What are the possible new grounds for dialogue, from my position at the margin, with architect colleagues?

Architecture without Building
Babar Khan Mumtaz

It was a 1964 exhibition at New York's Museum of Modern Art that made the case for *Architecture Without Architects* as an attempt 'to break down our narrow concepts of the art of building by introducing the unfamiliar world of non-pedigreed architecture'. In the accompanying book, the exhibition's curator, Austrian architect and author Bernard Rudofsky, also explored the idea of the anonymous architect and of '*communal* architecture – architecture produced not by specialists but by the spontaneous and continuing activity of a whole people with a common heritage, acting within a community of experience'.

Since then, greater awareness and understanding and a less ethnocentric world-view changed the way we see the sorts of structure that Rudofsky presented. Whether only qualified architects are capable of producing good architecture is now, of course, a question not even worth asking. Indeed, over the years, the Aga Khan Award for Architecture has been bestowed upon some projects built without the assistance of architects.

The Award is particularly cognizant of the fact that the production of a building or structure is rarely brought about by the architect without the support of at least a client and a contractor. This is particularly so in the case of projects that have received the Aga Khan Award, since they must have actually been constructed and in use for at least a year before they are eligible for the Award. In all the premiated projects, therefore, clients, sponsors, builders, engineers, contractors and craftspeople are recognized and acknowledged, along with designers.

The purpose of the Award in recognizing and rewarding excellence in architecture, however, is also to raise overall standards in the built environment, particularly in Islamic societies. It is in this context that it is worth considering the process of the production of architecture. While there can be no doubt that by far the greatest contribution is made by architects, designers and builders through the production of buildings, there are others who make a significant contribution to shaping, defining and developing architecture – and what is more, do so without building.

It is possible to identify a number of such producers of 'architecture without building', including educators, regulators, clients, financiers and the architect's peers, who together and separately operate to varying degrees in different countries and contexts. They affect and influence architecture as much as, and in some cases even more than, architects and designers do. They do so by defining and directing what can and cannot be designed or built, as well as the room for manoeuvre that architects and designers have. The fact that some architects will always manage to break loose and eventually help to reset the parameters does little to diminish the impact and influence of those who fashion architecture without building. This is the more so if by architecture we mean not just a building or even a group of buildings by an architect or group of architects, but the output of a society, a culture or a period. For such a wide interpretation it is necessary to take into account not just the gems but also the setting – and that setting is made up of buildings that owe much of their form, indeed their very existence, to the power and influence of those who produce architecture without building.

Regulators

Building and urban planning regulators have an obvious and immediate impact on what can and cannot be done. Established to protect society from the greed or ignorance of the individual, regulations also protect the individual from the excesses or arbitrary acts of the state, and the areas of construction that are subject to legal control are becoming ever more extensive and stringent.

The range of controls stretches from the aesthetic to the scientific – from what a building looks like to how it is constructed and of what materials. It is not only in areas that are of historical or aesthetic value that the appearance of buildings is subject to control. However, the more an area is acknowledged as exceptionally beautiful, the more such controls are accepted. Of course, that still begs the question of definition – both of what constitutes exceptional and what may be acceptable additions or modifications to such an environment. As such, there is always some room for interpretation and, therefore, subjectivity. To a greater or lesser degree, 'aesthetic' controls extend to all buildings, at least in urban areas, in all countries. At their least subjective such controls may be expressed and applied mechanically by 'non-negotiable' legislation; for example, limiting the height or extent of building development. Examples of the type 'no building [in Washington, D.C.,] shall be higher than the Capitol' may be found in any number of cities, particularly those keen to preserve their 'culture'. Less common are stipulations such as that by the Municipality of Amman, Jordan, that 'all buildings that are not built of [local] stone must be painted white'.

It was not long ago that, for most cities, there was no need to enact formal legislation to this effect, since the colour and appearance of most buildings was limited by what was locally available. If they were not to resort to enormous expense, most architects and their buildings had to make do with the same materials and, for the main part, were also limited by locally available techno-logies and skills. The resulting architecture had an inbuilt conformity. Importing materials, or architects for that matter, was an option available only to the very rich and therefore very powerful, who were usually literally beyond the law. Even if there had been aesthetic legislation, such clients could have escaped its controls. Now, few buildings can be built using locally available materials since even these need to be transported considerable distances in the bigger cities. And most buildings use manufactured materials that are transported great distances, if not imported from around the globe, with transport costs more than offset by cheaper production costs. In these circumstances, any attempt to control what buildings look like has to be made through formal legislation.

Over the years, most cities have come to incorporate, as a matter of course, some aesthetic concerns in their legislation to protect society from individual excesses. This is the case even with 'New Towns', which have nothing to preserve but seek to protect the future from the actions of the present. Precisely because there are problems of definition and interpretation, most architects, not surprisingly, are able to work with these regulations and even use them to good effect – sometimes as an ally to convince a client. In any case, such legislation is only as powerful as the society it serves, and in many societies most people overlook legislation. The rich can afford to flout such regulations – if for no other reason than to show that they can and to flaunt their wealth. The poor often cannot afford to comply with regulations, even if they are aware of them, and have so much else to worry about.

However, there are other areas of legislation that carry more weight. These are to do with health and safety, but have a bearing on what a building looks like, often explicitly so. Concerns about health first played an important part in legislation controlling buildings in the post-industrial cities of Britain. Appalled at the overcrowded tenements and afraid that the diseases spawned in the slums could easily spread to and affect the rich, the government regulated the layout and construction of buildings. The circulation of air was seen as the primary weapon in the fight against disease, not just at home but also in the British Empire. The ideal for the Englishman abroad was the bungalow, in splendid isolation from its neighbours and in stark contrast to the higgledy-piggledy housing of the natives. Even today, the bungalow – now renamed 'the villa' – is the building of choice in South Asia, and the courtyard house, so eminently suitable not just for the culture but also for the climate, cannot satisfy the regulatory criteria. Not only has this had a profound effect on the appearance of cities, especially residential areas, it has also affected lifestyles. Similarly, legislation regarding the size of fenestration often ignores climatic issues by stipulating oversized windows unsuitable for hot, dry conditions and glare.

Safety concerns underpin much of the legislation relating to the size and composition of the structure and materials of buildings, and rightly so. Nevertheless, there are often discrepancies between the intent and the impact. I remember sitting in the then newly built Architecture Faculty building in Kumasi, Ghana, as Buckminster Fuller made rapid-fire calculations and showed that it was some 3,000 times overdesigned! He cheated a bit, for he added together all of the cautious assumptions made by the legislation, but even so, the point he was making was valid and it is probably just as well that building regulations err on the side of safety. On the other hand, a study funded by the United States Agency for International Development in 2002 showed that out of the hundreds of building and planning regulations in Kenya, only six had any actual impact on health or safety. In practice, of course, the legislation ensures safety only to the extent it is applied, as the tragic consequences of the earthquakes in Izmit, Turkey, showed.

So, <u>since regulations have an impact on architecture, how is it possible to ensure that this impact is positive and that regulations are respected and applied</u>? Such issues arise only because the framing and policing of regulations are removed from society. <u>Ideally, regulations should reflect people's aspirations and respond to their needs and experience</u>. In the majority of countries in the developing world, building and planning legislation is imported wholesale, with little or no reference to society. If anything, the framing of legislation is seen as something that belongs solely to the technocratic domain. It should not be surprising, therefore, when 'ordinary people' find it incomprehensible why they should not build over the whole of their plots or paint their houses colourfully. Indeed it probably does not even occur to them that there is legislation that applies.

In Sri Lanka, when low-income communities were upgraded and improved, the residents were able to frame their own regulations for those aspects that did not affect the city or neighbouring communities. Together with facilitators from the National Housing Development Authority, they agreed on plot sizes, coverage, street setbacks, the provision of openings, respecting privacy, building height and other such matters that had an immediate impact on the look and feel of an area. This helped to produce not just a viable set of regulations, but also a community that understood and therefore respected and enforced them.

In Turkey, where most urban construction has a speculative element, even among lower-income housing, it has been suggested that a free service be offered to inspect, advise and, where satisfactory, certify that a building meets earthquake and disaster mitigation measures. Owners would be entitled to display a plaque in confirmation, which would add a premium to the sale price of apartments. Transforming compliance from an obligation to something desirable and providing a tangible symbol is felt to be far more effective than the present system, under which building regulation certification is seen as yet another bureaucratic expense.

Devolution, participation and facilitation (including explanation) are the key attributes for the development of building and planning legislation that is responsive, reflective and respected. This, of course, means a better-educated and informed bureaucracy and one that sees itself more as a facilitator than a regulator, inspector or enforcer.

Educators
For better or for worse, to practise architecture today requires formal architectural training, which has the potential for a major impact on the practice of architecture. It is in the nature of a profession such as architecture that the essential skill of design cannot be entirely taught but has to be developed. Many schools of architecture have stated that they do not see their job as producing architects, but rather as training problem-solvers. Those graduates that want to become architects are expected to acquire the professional skills they need as part of their work experience.

When these principles are extended to schools in developing countries and the architectural curriculum replicated, they fail. They fail for the same reason industrialization failed to provide development: most developing countries set up factories but were unable to set up industries, where industry means not just the unit of production (the factory) but the whole chain of upstream and downstream suppliers and consumers that are needed for the transformation from raw commodity to finished product. Architects in these countries, fresh out of school, jump into the deep end without an appropriate period of apprenticeship and start operating without a support infrastructure. When these architects constitute the bulk of the profession and take on the training of the next generation, architecture enters a downward spiral.

Most architecture schools have a very tenuous link with practice; some go so far as to prohibit their staff from undertaking any architectural work. Nor do they compensate by using practising architects to provide input to the teaching. Most courses then become endless repetitions of what the teacher once learned. Perhaps the most glaring omission from most architectural education is any introduction to or familiarity with the current architecture of the country in question. Architectural history and criticism are alien concepts, separated by space and time from current realities and therefore unable to provide any insights into the future development of architecture.

Currently, most schools of architecture and their staff see themselves as teaching just another academic discipline and model themselves on university departments as far as their structure, teaching methods, admissions and exam-ination procedures are concerned. They tend to ignore their responsibilities, not just to the profession but also as academics; little or no research and scholarship are built into the curriculum or incorporated into staff development.

For architectural education to provide the training and skill development required for the production and sustenance of appropriate architecture, schools of architecture have to realize that their responsibilities include the development of a profession. This will require not just more professionally able educators but also a more professionally oriented curriculum. That in turn must be grounded in research, particularly into current practice and issues affecting architecture in the country in question. This shift, indeed transformation, is unlikely to be accomplished without assistance. Particularly the schools in the smaller countries are going to find it very difficult to recruit and retain adequately qualified staff. Perhaps a system of regional, peripatetic staffing will have to be considered, with schools making joint appointments of staff who can service their needs by teaching at several schools in rotation. At the same time, scholarship and research among architects – in particular the promotion of critical judgement and discourse – will have to be initiated. Again, it is difficult in small societies to avoid being seen as personally motivated or biased, and a regional outlook may go down better in an environment unused to critical appraisal.

Architects, clients and others
Architects obviously affect and influence architecture, even when they are not building. Indeed, it might be argued that their influence may be even greater when they are not building! Architects have always explored alternatives and experimented with innovative solutions through 'projects' that not only never get built but may not even be intended to be built. An architect that waits for a commission may well have a long wait, and even when there is a client, the brief may be too restrictive to explore non-conventional ideas, especially for a young

architect at the beginning of his or her career. Le Corbusier and Mies van der Rohe were arguably at their most inventive when designing theoretical projects – as, more recently, have been Archigram, Rem Koolhaas and Zaha Hadid, to name but three – extending the frontiers of architecture and creating a style without building. The process is facilitated by the architectural press and by architectural historians and critics. Charles Jencks was largely instrumental in transforming the work of architects into Postmodernism through writing and not by building.

The Internet and the development of the virtual gallery has made it possible for artists to display and sell their work and win commissions from clients. But the use of this medium by architects to publish their work and broadcast their ideas is still in its infancy, though computerization has made it easier for them to demonstrate their ideas and put on a convincing show for their clients. The use of three-dimensional renderings and 'walk-throughs' is especially valuable for a client unused to reading plans and elevations.

The combination of an architectural press, critical analysis, ideas competitions and architects using hypothetical projects seems to be missing in most developing countries. As a result there is far less innovation or interpretation of what architecture could and should be in these places. In the absence of such resources locally, young architects turn to international sources for inspiration and indeed validation of their own work.

Unless they can showcase their ideas, architects are likely to be restricted to following rather than setting the style. This makes it more difficult for architects to educate their clients as to what could be possible, and leaves many architects complaining that the quality of their work is poor because of what their clients want. This may be feeble, but has certainly led some clients to echo the view of the chairman of the Water and Power Development Corporation, the largest commissioner of civil works in Pakistan: 'Architects are a luxury that developing countries such as Pakistan cannot afford.'

Conclusion
More concerted action must be taken to address directly the operation and outlook of some of the actors and agencies that influence and create architecture without building. This would reinforce the aspirations of the Aga Khan Award for Architecture to inspire and encourage the development of architectural excellence in the Muslim world.

A Breakthrough
Suha Özkan

Awards are important honours that validate the accomplishments of architectural professionals and make their contributions more widely known to the general public. Such awards may recognize the lifelong commitment of notable architects or recognize individual, new and exemplary works of architecture or planning. The Aga Khan Award for Architecture has recognized three Muslims for their outstanding lifetime achievements in architecture,[1] but seeks primarily to pay tribute to projects of merit that indicate directions for positive future change.

Each triennial cycle of the Award yields new and fresh thinking for improving the environments primarily, but not exclusively, of Muslims. An understanding of the values of plurality and coexistence has characterized the Award and the Master Juries' decisions ever since the announcement of the first cycle of the Award in 1980. Since then, eighty-five projects, covering a wide spectrum of architecture, landscape design and urban improvement, have received Awards. Each cyclical Jury identifies contributions in architecture that respond to the priorities of the present time. The seven projects identified by the current Master Jury make further contributions to some of these areas, but more notably represent international architectural standards of the highest quality.

The collective profile of the 2004 Aga Khan Awards might be grouped under three headings: heritage and conservation, exploration and experimentation, and large-scale innovation. Two projects exemplify the importance of conserving historic architectural heritage in the Muslim world: the restoration of Al-Abbas Mosque● near the village of Asnaf, Yemen, and the Old City of Jerusalem Revitalization Programme.● Three of the projects place emphasis on the importance of exploration and experimentation in architecture: the Gando Primary School● in Burkina Faso, the B2 House● in the rural village of Ayvacık, Turkey, and the Sandbag Shelter Prototypes● for the provision of housing in emergency situations. Finally, the two remaining projects – Bibliotheca Alexandrina● in Alexandria,

The Chairman's Award has been presented in recognition of the lifetime achievement of a Muslim architect on three occasions:

to Hassan Fathy in 1980,

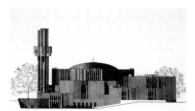

Rifat Chadirji in 1986,

and Geoffrey Bawa in 2001.

2

Ali Qapu, Chehel Sutun and Hasht Behesht, Isfahan, Iran, 1980

Ertegün House, Bodrum, Turkey, 1980

National Museum, Doha, Qatar, 1980

Rüstem Paşa Caravanserai, Edirne, Turkey, 1980

Azem Palace, Damascus, Syria, 1983

Tomb of Shah Rukn-i-'Alam,
Multan, Pakistan, 1983

Al-Aqsa Mosque, al-Haram
al-Sharif, Jerusalem, 1986

Historic Sites Development,
Istanbul, Turkey, 1986

Great Omari Mosque, Sidon,
Lebanon, 1989

Egypt, and the Petronas Towers ● in Kuala Lumpur, Malaysia – are large-scale projects characterized by innovative technological advances and striking architectural symbolism.

Heritage and conservation

The conservation and protection of the extraordinary architectural heritage of Muslim societies have been vivid concerns for all of the successive Award Master Juries. During recent cycles, emphasis has been placed on those projects that not only show the highest standards of international conservation, but that also ensure the continuing use and vibrancy of examples of architectural legacy as important components of contemporary life.[2]

In the current cycle, the restoration of Al-Abbas Mosque ● brings a new dimension of accomplishment to the field of conservation. Although work concentrated on one small but highly significant and symbolic edifice, dramatically sited in the rugged mountains of the Yemeni landscape, the project permitted further training of already highly skilled Yemeni craftsmen, while reinforcing the social cohesion of the communities residing near the mosque. The work was undertaken with meticulous care and dedicated effort and conviction. The painstaking perseverance of the restorers was at times adversely affected by political turmoil and national unease during the ten-year period in which the restoration was undertaken. However, these unfavourable conditions did not daunt the restorers or any of the many contributors to the project. As a result of over a decade of effort, the jewel-like monument has once again regained its place as one of the most important examples of world architectural heritage.

A key aspect of this project was its strict observance of international standards of restoration. As much original material as possible was maintained and carefully restored; in places where new elements were required, special care was given to their craftsmanship and to identifying them clearly as non-original. Research and training were major components of the endeavour, based on a conviction that the efforts invested in this singular building could be followed in other buildings throughout Yemen and the region.

The protection and conservation of cities throughout the Muslim world have also drawn the attention of the Award Master Juries, beginning with the village of Sidi Bou Saïd in Tunisia, which received an Award in 1980, and leading to the recognition of the Old City of Jerusalem Revitalization Programme, ● which is being honoured during the present cycle.[3]

The complexity of urban conservation varies from one culture to another and also differs greatly in terms of building technology and the techniques required for restoration. The economic and social aspects of conservation require particularly creative solutions for financing and to foster cultural relativity.

The Old City of Jerusalem Revitalization Programme ● is notable for being a genuinely integrated programme. It includes not only housing but also

3

Conservation of Sidi Bou Saïd,
Tunis, Tunisia, 1980

Darb Qirmiz Quarter, Cairo,
Egypt, 1983

Conservation of Mostar Old Town,
Bosnia-Herzegovina, 1986

Rehabilitation of Asilah,
Morocco, 1989

Kairouan Conservation Programme,
Tunisia, 1992

Conservation of Old Sana'a,
Yemen, 1995

Reconstruction of Hafsia Quarter II,
Tunis, Tunisia, 1995

Restoration of Bukhara Old City,
Uzbekistan, 1995

Rehabilitation of Hebron Old Town,
1998

New Life for Old Structures in
various locations, Iran, 2001

community buildings and the enhancement of urban life. Thus a school, a nursery, a meeting facility, a library and a restaurant have all been provided, along with housing, which has been restored for the comfort and well-being of more than ninety families. The restoration techniques employed and the degree to which recuperation of the original buildings has been accomplished are based on the social and economic realities that prevail in this part of Jerusalem. It is an important objective and achievement of the programme that the houses and community facilities have been restored to accommodate the urgent and immediate needs of the resident families, rather than to gentrify the area for higher-income groups.

The Swiss-based Welfare Association, an international non-governmental organization, centrally finances the revitalization. By receiving funds from a central source, the restorers are able to maintain the highest quality of conservation and restoration – stringent international standards outlined by the Venice Charter are consistently observed throughout.

The Old City of Jerusalem Revitalization Programme● also features strong components for research, publications, teaching and training. It thus aims not only to undertake physical restoration, but also to inform the wider public. While many conservation efforts elsewhere yield important but highly technical and academic literature, the generation and wide dissemination of easily accessible information is at the heart of the Jerusalem project. This permits residents to contribute to and understand the overall process and long-term objectives, while allowing funders, donors and others interested in the work to follow closely the progress of the project, including the expenditure of funds. The Jerusalem revitalization project● will require the work of many future generations; today, it continues to make exemplary progress under stringent and difficult circumstances.

Exploration and experimentation

The Award Master Juries have always encouraged the use of appropriate technologies, combined with local materials. During the very first Award cycle, in 1980, the legacy of the late Hassan Fathy (1900–89) was singled out for the first Chairman's Award. His example of helping people to build for themselves, using local materials and traditional techniques, continues to be of great importance and influence the world over. The creativity of architects in developing alternative technologies and expressions of built form has also been a strong feature in every cycle of the Aga Khan Award.[4] Most examples have represented the confirmed application of new procedures and new materials, but for this cycle of the Award, the Master Jury has selected a powerful prototype that has not yet been fully developed or applied.

The Sandbag Shelter Prototypes⬤ employ raw earth or sand – readily and cheaply avail-able nearly everywhere – as the principal construction material. Earth or sand is compacted manually into plastic or jute bags, which are stacked cylindrically to create parabolic domed spaces; strands of barbed wire are laid between each layer to hold them in place. The rooms can be modified and expanded according to the needs or means of the users to create additional space or auxiliary service areas. Initial results have shown that the sustainability of the Sandbag Shelter is more promising than nearly all other techniques.

Packing loose granular material within tensile envelopes is a well-known practice in architecture and engineering, used especially in road construction to contain gravel and stones as protective barriers against landslides. However, the proto-type Sandbag Shelter is perhaps the first demonstration of the use of sand or earth without any binding element, such as cement, and the technology provides simple but effective resistance against lateral forces, including those resulting from earthquakes. The prototype has been tested in several parts of the world as temporary housing for victims of natural disasters and for refugees. The technique requires no skilled labour and only minimal materials from outside sources. As such, the Sandbag Shelter offers great possibilities for future use.

The Gando Primary School⬤ in Burkina Faso, addresses the specific conditions of the rural village in which it is located, but contains strong potential for replication elsewhere due to the intelligence and innovation of its architecture. Diébédo Francis Kéré, the son of the village chief, studied architecture in Germany, where he learned the skills and techniques of his profession. He was the first member of his village to undertake higher education abroad. Aware of, and grateful for, the benefits of this opportunity, he became convinced that education is essential to human development, and sought to combine this conviction with the architectural talents he had acquired in order to create a new school for the children of his village. He was guided by the dual faith that architecture can provide a nurturing environment and that education can be enhanced by the architectural quality of schools.

The components of Kéré's project are simple, functional and driven by reality, and they demonstrate good design. He conceived the architecture of the school in three layers. The lowest level is a platform paved with hexagonal bricks; this plinth consolidates the foundation and serves to protect the building from dust, sand and water. The top level is a corrugated steel cover, placed over rudimentary triangular trusses in steel that form a simple space frame. The space between

Agricultural Training Centre, Nianing, Senegal, 1980

Sidi el-Aloui Primary School, Tunis, Tunisia, 1989

Stone Building System, Dar'a Province, Syria, 1992

A Breakthrough • Architecture and Polyphony

the corrugated shield and the ceiling of the building below is left open to permit continuous circulation of air and to protect against radiant heat. Three large classrooms are located between the protective layers of the roof and base, interspersed with large, covered, open areas used both for recreation and teaching. The main structure comprises load-bearing walls made from locally produced compressed-earth bricks; concrete is used only for the beams that support the ceilings.

Kéré showed imagination and determination in obtaining financing for the project, as well. With a group of friends, he set up a fund-raising organization in Germany and also secured the assistance of a government company in Burkina Faso to provide training in the manufacture of compressed, stabilized earth bricks. All of the community members of the village of Gando – young and old, male and female – were motivated to contribute in any manner they could, and they participated in the entire construction process. The Gando Primary School represents a breakthrough, applying admirable design skills to provide an elegant building made of local materials and to bring a sense of achievement and hope to an entire village.

Throughout architectural history, the design and construction of private residences have provided architects with opportunities and inspiration for innovation and experiment. In almost every cycle of the Award, the Jury selections have included private houses that demonstrate a high degree of architectural achievement – often the result of experimentation with intellectual ideas and technological advances nurtured by the dreams and ideals of architects.[5]

For the 2004 Award Cycle, a minimalist summer residence in Ayvacık, a rural Turkish village set in a sloping Aegean landscape, has been selected to receive an Award. The B2 House, commissioned by two brothers, consists of two zones. The first, narrower zone faces a hillside and encompasses all of the house's service spaces. The second zone is fronted by open terraces giving views onto the surrounding landscape and sea. The main living space is located on a lower level, while the upper level has two bedrooms. To emphasize the simplicity – perhaps austerity – of the design, the staircase connecting the two levels is placed on the exterior of the house, but also used to create additional outdoor spaces that are an integral part of the design. The house features an extraordinary combination of indoor and outdoor spaces and a keen understanding of climate and environmental control through such effective but simple elements as reed-panel sunscreens. The project is an inspiring example of the minimalist design ideology of the architect, Han Tümertekin, working closely with the clients, two cosmopolitan and sophisticated brothers who appreciate the value of architectural experimentation.

In the discouraging context of opulence and abuse of building materials that characterizes so many private residences in contemporary societies, this house was achieved at a medium cost and affirms the inherent beauty of the surfaces and textures of exposed concrete, untreated stone and simple natural materials. It remains distant from, and yet at the same time perfectly integrated into, the village of which it forms a part.

5

Halawa House, Agamy, Egypt, 1980

Nail Çakırhan Residence, Akyaka Village, Turkey, 1983

Ramses Wissa Wassef Arts Centre, Giza, Egypt, 1983

Gürel Family Summer Residence, Çanakkale, Turkey, 1989

Salinger Residence, Selangor, Malaysia, 1998

Large-scale innovation

The iconography of large-scale buildings, whether government, public or corporate structures, elicits an opinion, or a fleeting impression at least, from nearly everyone. Over time, many such buildings become symbols in the popular imagination and represent the aspirations of entire communities and even nations. These large facilities are also the workspaces of thousands of people who are directly affected by the quality of architecture and the working conditions the buildings provide. Large-scale buildings have featured in each Award cycle.[6] Fine works by some of the world's greatest architects are included in this group and, in the 2004 Award Cycle, two additional large-scale edifices are celebrated.

The ancient Library of Alexandria was the world's most important centre of learning. Destroyed by fire, the original library – even its ruins – has now disappeared, though its legend remains vivid in the collective memory. A noble initiative of the Egyptian government to revive the institution garnered worldwide support, and the new Bibliotheca Alexandrina ● is one of the most important buildings of recent decades. The project was the result of an international competition and the completed building is the collaborative product of a multinational team.

In spite of its massive volume, the eleven-storey building fits well into the city of Alexandria. Inside, the memorable main reading room is divided by steps and terraces into distinct reading areas and shelf spaces, so that it cascades down towards the Mediterranean Sea, creating an exhilarating and dramatic spatial experience. A stone-clad exterior wall encircles the building and brings unity to the large complex. The stone facing is carved with characters drawn from all the alphabets of the world, further enhancing the symbolism of this unique centre of learning.

The transverse cross-section of the building can be seen as a terraced wedge that ascends from levels devoted to fields of basic knowledge to the topmost level, featuring the most recent developments of the electronic era. An exhibition gallery and auxiliary spaces are located beneath the wedge. The modular roof panelling has a well-proportioned amount of glazing that draws a comfortable amount of northern light into the reading areas from above. Bibliotheca Alexandrina ● symbolizes many of the world's most treasured values of learning and history and, at the same time, is a dramatic confirmation of the potential of today's architecture.

The other large-scale facility awarded this cycle is a high-rise, multi-use centre in Kuala Lumpur, the Petronas Towers. ● The towers are the second tallest buildings in the world, and represent one of many significant techno-logical advances recognized by the Award since its inception in 1977.[7] The Petronas Towers taper at the top, making efficient use of the lower floors and foundations. While it is common practice to use steel for the main structure of high-rise buildings, the Petronas Towers were built with high-performance reinforced concrete, which is more resistant to fire and other hazards. The forms of the floor plans are derived from a polygonal geometry with sixteen angles and

Intercontinental Hotel and Conference Centre, Mecca, Saudi Arabia, 1980

Ministry of Foreign Affairs, Riyadh, Saudi Arabia, 1989

National Assembly Building, Sher-e-Bangla Nagar, Dhaka, Bangladesh, 1989

Entrepreneurship Development Institute of India, Ahmedabad, India, 1992

Alhambra Arts Council, Lahore, Pakistan, 1998

Vidhan Bhavan, Bhopal, India, 1998

Water Towers, Kuwait City, Kuwait, 1980

Hajj Terminal, King Abdul Aziz International Airport, Jeddah, Saudi Arabia, 1983

Institut du Monde Arabe, Paris, France, 1989

Menara Mesiniaga, Kuala Lumpur, Malaysia, 1995

Tuwaiq Palace, Riyadh, Saudi Arabia, 1998

lobes, and the circular and triangular projections offer many possibilities for furnishing, while also providing daylight for the interior workspaces. Cross-beams spanning each floor permit a maximum amount of undivided floor space. The innovative structural system is pioneering, and the construction was entirely Malaysian.

Contemporary Malaysia is a rich fabric of many different cultures with a predominantly Muslim population. The country is an exemplary model of pluralism, with a commitment to respecting and enhancing the beliefs and mores of all its citizens, while placing an emphasis on modernity and progress. This unique context permits projects such as the Petronas Towers to flourish.

Lacunae

One of the hallmarks of the Award is the acknow-ledgement that no group of winning projects can fully address the many issues, themes and needs that are current in contemporary Islamic societies. It is the cumulative breadth of the premiated projects that constitutes the Award's message and legacy.

In the current cycle, examples of important urban interventions aimed at improving the architectural and environmental conditions of existing de facto or informal communities have not come forward, as they have in the past.[8] Neither do the winning projects of this cycle encompass solutions for the housing crisis growing in the Islamic world, though such solutions have previously been prominent.[9] Former cycles have also included housing as a key feature of some excellent examples of rural development, including the innovative Grameen Bank programme for rural housing in Bangladesh, which has provided over 100,000 safe dwellings for rural families and is probably the Award's most important contribution in the field of housing.[10]

Every year, tens of thousands of mosques are built, but sadly very few demonstrate any architectural excellence or quality. No contemporary mosques or religious facilities are included in the winning projects this cycle, although the Old City of Jerusalem Revitalization Programme● and Al-Abbas Mosque●

Kampung Improvement Programme, Jakarta, Indonesia, 1980

Pondok Pesantren Pabelan, Central Java, Indonesia, 1980

Ismaïliyya Development Projects, Ismaïliyya, Egypt, 1986

Kampung Kebalen Improvement, Surabaya, Indonesia, 1986

East Wahdat Upgrading Programme, Amman, Jordan, 1992

9

Kampung Kali Cho-de, Yogyakarta, Indonesia, 1992

Khuda-ki-Basti Incremental Development Scheme, Hyderabad, Pakistan, 1995

Courtyard Houses, Agadir, Morocco, 1980

Hafsia Quarter, Tunis, Tunisia, 1983

Slum Networking of Indore City, India, 1998

Shushtar New Town, Shushtar, Iran, 1986

Dar Lamane Housing Community, Casablanca, Morocco, 1986

Aranya Community Housing, Indore, India, 1995

11

Great Mosque of Niono, Mali, 1983

Sherefudin's White Mosque, Visoko, Bosnia-Herzegovina, 1983

Bhong Mosque, Rahim-Yar Khan, Pakistan, 1986

10

Grameen Bank Housing Programme, various locations, Bangladesh, 1989

Aït Iktel, Abadou, Morocco, 2001

Barefoot Architects, Tilonia, India, 2001

Kahere Eila Poultry Farming School, Koliagbe, Guinea, 2001

Saïd Naum Mosque, Jakarta, Indonesia, 1986

Yaama Mosque, Tahoua, Niger, 1986

Corniche Mosque, Jeddah, Saudi Arabia, 1989

Great Mosque of Riyadh and Redevelopment of the Old City Centre, Saudi Arabia, 1995

Mosque of the Grand National Assembly, Ankara, Turkey, 1995

are fine examples of the restoration of historic mosques. Places of worship demand a sense of spirituality, with qualities of light and space that express their special nature. Some of these qualities are represented in the mosques that have been selected to receive Aga Khan Awards in the past, which display a wide spectrum of architectural expression, from traditional to popular, from regionalist to contemporary.[11]

The Award has also made efforts to seek out excellent architecture in health facilities, but to date the Master Juries have not identified any fully functioning hospitals in dense urban centres. Hospitals are among the most technically challenging and complex building types, but this should not preclude innovative architectural solutions in their design. While clinics and a small hospital figure among the projects premiated in past Award cycles,[12] larger hospitals and healthcare facilities still require attention from the Award nominators in order to highlight the importance of this specialized domain.

Industrial facilities are absent from the winning projects this cycle once again, though the Award Steering Committee has drawn attention to this and other fields through correspondence with over a thousand nominators who suggest the building projects to be considered by the Master Jury. Since 1977, when the Aga Khan founded the Award, successive Steering Committees have continued their search for industrial facilities that demonstrate architectural excellence. To date, however, these efforts have not succeeded, and no industrial project has ever been identified to receive an Award. Still, the quality of work environments, where most of us spend the greatest portion of our lives, deserves more attention and better examples to guide the industrialists, investors and decision-makers who constitute the clients. Two projects selected to receive Awards this cycle – the Petronas Towers● and Bibliotheca Alexandrina● – do, however, show good signs for the provision of excellent workspaces in contemporary facilities.

Perhaps the most interesting surprise of the Ninth Cycle of the Award is the absence of projects that represent 'regionalist' architecture. In the past, the

[12]

Medical Centre, Mopti, Mali, 1980

Kaedi Regional Hospital, Kaedi, Mauritania, 1995

Lepers Hospital, Chopda Taluka, India, 1998

selections of Award Juries have always included examples of regionalism. Among many distinguished contributors, the most noteworthy proponents of this tradition in architecture are Alvar Aaalto of Finland, Luis Barragán of Mexico and Alvaro Siza of Portugal, to name only three. Regionalism in architecture searches for deep roots into history, professes the relevance of cultural identity, and is particularly sensitive to climatic conditions. Even though it can sometimes be characterized by an excessive use of derivative vernacular or traditional forms and expressions, regionalism is in many respects the search for authentic modern expressions that are relevant to context. Different architects give different interpretations to context, some defining it by culture, others by climate, and still others by architectural expression. Many of these approaches have been recognized by the Award in influential projects by Charles Correa and Balkrishna Doshi of India; Nayyar Ali Dada of Pakistan; Rasem Badran and Jafar Tukan from Jordan; Ali Shuaibi and Basem Shihabi from Saudi Arabia; Sedad Eldem, Turgut Cansever, Cengiz Bektaş and Sedat Gürel from Turkey; Serge Santelli from France; and Jimmy C.S. Lim and Kerry Hill from Malaysia.[13]

Finally, another conspicuous absence this cycle is the category of open spaces. It is a common concern that environmental degradation and damage is taking place throughout Muslim societies, and this is a worry for everyone throughout the world. Parks, plazas, playgrounds and pedestrian areas are – unlike buildings – not for limited users, but are for the benefit of all. In the past, Award Juries have recognized many extraordinary and exemplary accomplishments in urban contexts, and most have become models of quality for others to follow. [14]

Let us hope that future cycles of the Award will discover exemplary projects to address these and other areas of concern.

13

Mughal Sheraton Hotel, Agra, India, 1980

Turkish Historical Society, Ankara, Turkey, 1980

Résidence Andalous, Sousse, Tunisia, 1983

Tanjong Jara Beach Hotel and Rantau Abang Visitors' Centre, Kuala Terengganu, Malaysia, 1983

Social Security Complex, Istanbul, Turkey, 1986

Al-Kindi Plaza, Riyadh, Saudi Arabia, 1989

Demir Holiday Village, Bodrum, Turkey, 1992

Panafrican Institute for Development, Ouagadougou, Burkina Faso, 1992

Alliance Franco-Sénégalaise, Kaolack, Senegal, 1995

Datai Hotel, Pulau Langkawi, Malaysia, 2001

14

Citra Niaga Urban Development, Samarinda, East Kalimantan, Indonesia, 1989

Hayy Assafarat Landscaping, Riyadh, Saudi Arabia, 1989

Cultural Park for Children, Cairo, Egypt, 1992

Palace Parks Programme, Istanbul, Turkey, 1992

Landscaping Integration of the Soekarno-Hatta Airport, Cengkareng, Indonesia, 1995

Nubian Museum, Aswan, Egypt, 2001

Olbia Social Centre, Akdeniz Üniversitesi, Antalya, Turkey, 2001

Reforestation Programme of the Middle East Technical University, Ankara, Turkey, 1995

SOS Children's Village, Aqaba, Jordan, 2001

Bagh-e-Ferdowsi, Tehran, Iran, 2001

Akram Abu Hamdan is a Jordanian architect, trained at the Architectural Association School of Architecture in London. Mr Abu Hamdan directed an architectural research unit at Jordan's Royal Scientific Society from 1979 to 1982, and has been a lecturer and design tutor at the University of Jordan School of Architecture. In private practice in Amman, Mr Abu Hamdan's work has focused on architectural themes that support vibrant urban spaces. He has been a council member of the Greater Amman Municipality and coordinator for a documentation study of the old city of Jerusalem conducted jointly by Harvard University and the Royal Scientific Society of Jordan. Mr Abu Hamdan served as Commissioner General and Chairman of the Jordan National Committee for Expo 2000 in Hanover, as well as leading the design team of the Jordan Pavilion at the Expo, for which he was awarded the Medal of Independence by HM King Abdullah II. He is currently Director General of the National Resources Investment and Development Corporation, with responsibility for major urban regeneration projects in the cities of Amman, Zarqa and Aqaba. He is also Chairman of the Executive Committee for the Martyrs Memorial Public Park Project in Amman, and Commisioner General for Jordan for the Expo 2005 World Exposition to be held in Aichi, Japan. Mr Abu Hamdan served as a Technical Reviewer during the 2001 Award Cycle.

Charles Correa is an Indian architect, planner, activist and theoretician who studied architecture at the Massachusetts Institute of Technology (MIT), Cambridge, Massachusetts, and the University of Michigan, Ann Arbor. He has taught and lectured at many universities, both in India and abroad, including MIT, Harvard, the University of London, and Cambridge University, where he was Nehru Professor. Mr Correa is known for the wide range of his architectural projects in India and for his work on urbanization and low-cost shelter in the Third World, which he articulated in his 1985 publication, *The New Landscape*. His architectural designs have been internationally acclaimed and he has received many awards including the Royal Institute of British Architects Gold Medal (1984), the Indian Institute of Architects Gold Medal (1987), the International Union of Architects Gold Medal (1990), and the Praemium Imperiale for Architecture from the Japan Art Association (1994). Professor Correa was a member of the 1980, 1983, 1986 and 2001 Award Steering Committees, and of the 1989 Award Master Jury. He was presented an Aga Khan Award for Architecture during the 1998 cycle as the architect of Vidhan Bhavan in Bhopal, India.

Abdou Filali-Ansary is a Moroccan social scientist and Director of the Institute for the Study of Muslim Civilizations, Aga Khan University, London. Before he took up this post he was Director of the King Abdul-Aziz Al Saud Foundation for Islamic Studies and Human Sciences in Casablanca. Dr Filali-Ansary obtained a doctorate in philosophy from the University of Dijon in 1970 on the topic of 'The Notion of Intuition in the Philosophy of Spinoza and Bergson'. He has taught philosophy at the University of Rabat and served as Secretary General of the University of Mohamed V in Rabat. Since 1994 he has been the editor of *Prologues*, a scholarly journal devoted to literature and ideas of interest to the Maghrib. Dr Filali-Ansary has published numerous articles on contemporary Islamic thought, including 'The Challenge of Secularization' (*The Journal of Democracy*, Washington, D.C., 1996) and 'Islam and Secularization' (*Revista de Occident*, Madrid, 1997). His monograph entitled *Is Islam Hostile to Secularism?* was published in 1996. Dr Filali-Ansary was a member of the 2001 Award Master Jury.

Jacques Herzog is a Swiss architect and partner in the firm Herzog & de Meuron, recipients of the 2001 Pritzker Architecture Prize. Trained in architecture at the Swiss Federal Institute of Technology (ETH) in Zürich, Mr Herzog opened his private practice with Pierre de Meuron in Basle in 1978. Current and recent projects include the New de Young Museum in San Francisco (2005), the Prada Flagship Store in Tokyo (2003), the Laban Dance Centre in London (2003), the New Link Quay in Santa Cruz de Tenerife (2005), the Forum 2004 Building and Plaza in Barcelona (2004), and the Beijing National Stadium (2008). Following on the success of the St Jakob Park Stadium in Basle, Herzog & de Meuron are planning a new soccer stadium for Munich, to be inaugurated with the 2006 World Championships. The projects and completed work of Herzog & de Meuron are widely exhibited and published and featured in numerous monographs and catalogues. Mr Herzog is a visiting professor at Harvard Design School and co-founder of the ETH Studio Basel, Institute for the Contemporary City.

Glenn Lowry is an art historian from the United States and Director of the Museum of Modern Art (MoMA) in New York City. Among the major exhibitions that have taken place during Mr Lowry's tenure at MoMA are 'Matisse.Picasso' (2003), 'Mies in Berlin' (2001), 'Andreas Gursky' (2001), 'Workspheres' (2001), 'Jackson Pollock' (1998–99), 'Pierre Bonnard' (1998), 'Aleksandr Rodchenko' (1998), 'Chuck Close' (1998), 'Jasper Johns' (1996–97), 'Picasso and Portraiture' (1996) and 'Piet Mondrian' (1995). A noted scholar of Islamic arts and architecture, Mr Lowry was Director of the Art Gallery of Ontario from 1990 to 1995. From 1984 to 1990 he was Curator of Near Eastern Art at the Smithsonian Institution's Arthur M. Sackler Gallery and Freer Gallery of Art, where he organized, among other exhibitions, 'Timur and the Princely Vision: Persian Art and Culture in the Fifteenth Century' (1989) and 'A Jeweler's Eye: Islamic Arts of the Book From the Vever Collection' (1988). Mr Lowry's many honours include an honorary doctorate of fine arts from the Pennsylvania Academy of Fine Arts (2000), the Chevalier d'Ordre de Merite (2001) and Officier de l'Ordre des Arts et Lettres (2004) from the French government, and the Smithsonian Institution Scholarly Studies Award (1990).

Mohsen Mostafavi is an Iranian architect and Dean of the College of Architecture, Art and Planning at Cornell University in New York state. Mr Mostafavi received a diploma in architecture from the Architectural Association in London in 1976 and undertook research on Counter-Reformation urban history at the University of Essex and at Cambridge University. From 1995 to 2004 he was Chairman of the Architectural Association School of Architecture, and before that he was Director of the Master of Architecture 1 Program at the Graduate School of Design, Harvard University. Mr Mostafavi has also taught at the University of Pennsylvania, Cambridge University and Frankfurt Academy of Fine Arts. His research has been published in many journals, including *The Architectural Review, AA Files, Arquitectura, Bauwelt, Casabella, Centre* and *Daidalos*. He is co-author of *Architecture and Continuity* (with Dalibor Vesely, 1983), *Delayed Space* (with Homa Fardjadi, 1994) and *On Weathering: The Life of Buildings in Time* (with David Leatherbarrow, 1993), which received the American Institute of Architects Commendation Prize for writing on architectural theory. Mr Mostafavi's recent publications include: *Approximations* (2002) and *Surface Architecture* (2002).

Babar Khan Mumtaz is a reader in Housing Studies at the University of London and director of the Development Planning Unit at the Bartlett School of the Built Environment, London. Originally from Pakistan, Mr Mumtaz is a specialist in urban planning, housing and development and is committed to the improvement of living conditions in underprivileged societies. He has undertaken projects and led research throughout the world, including the Indian subcontinent, Central Asia, the Arab states, West Africa and the Pacific rim. He has also served as a consultant to a large number of national governments, international agencies and non-governmental organizations. Equally influential as a teacher, he has pioneered and contributed to the development of curricula for studies in development planning, urban housing, urban design in developing societies, and disaster management and preparedness, all with a focus on field experience for students to complement their academic studies. His writings on these topics are widely published, including *Meeting Housing Demand: A Model for Establishing Affordability Parameters for Housing* (1995) and *The Housing Question, and Other Answers* (with R. Ali, 1989). He is a frequent speaker at international meetings and scholarly conferences.

Peter G. Rowe is the Raymond Garbe Professor of Architecture and Urban Design at Harvard University, and Education Programme Director of the Aga Khan Trust for Culture. He served as Dean of the Graduate School of Design at Harvard from 1992 to 2004. Prior to joining the Harvard faculty in 1985, Professor Rowe was Director of the School of Architecture at Rice University, Houston, and a senior member of several research organizations, including the Rice Center and the Southwest Center for Urban Research, both in Houston. He is the author of numerous articles, principally concerned with matters of cultural interpretation and design in both architecture and urban design, as well as the relationship of urban form to issues of economic development, housing provision and resource conservation. Professor Rowe is also the author of many books, including *Modernity and Housing* (1993), *Civic Realism* (1997), *Projecting Beirut* (1998), *L'Asia e il Moderno* (1999), *Architectural Encounters with Essence and Form in Modern China* (2002), and *Shanghai: Making the Modern Metropolis* (2004).

2004 Award Master Jury

Ghada Amer is an Egyptian artist who lives and works in New York City. She trained at the École des Beaux-Arts in Nice, the School of the Museum of Fine Arts in Boston, and the Institut des Hautes Études en Arts Plastiques in Paris. Ms Amer's works include embroidered canvases, textile installations and sculptures, frequently incorporating imagery and texts reflecting on childhood, dreams, daily life, beauty, popular culture and sexuality. Her work is a synthesis of both Western and Eastern traditions and questions the role of women in contemporary societies. The pieces also examine gender-based stereotypes, as well as dispelling preconceived ideas and redefining the distinction between high and low forms of art, art and handicraft, East and West, male and female. Ms Amer's work has been presented in numerous solo shows and group exhibitions at museums and galleries throughout the United States, Europe and the Muslim world.

Hanif Kara is a London-based structural engineer originally from Uganda. Co-founder of the firm Adams Kara Taylor – a progressive, design-led structural and civil engineering consultancy in London – Mr Kara is particularly interested in innovative form, the use of new materials, prefabrication, sustainable construction, and complex form-finding and analysis methods. He has collaborated on numerous important and award-winning projects, such as Peckham Library in London (2000) (winner of the Stirling Prize), and has worked with leading architects and designers throughout the world, including Alsop Architects, Foreign Office Architects, Foster and Partners, Rafael Viñoly, and Zaha Hadid Architects. Mr Kara is a co-tutor for a design unit at the Architectural Association in London and has been visiting tutor at universities in Vienna and Stockholm. He is also an examiner for the Institution of Structural Engineers and a member of the Design Review Panel at the Commission for Architecture in the Built Environment (CABE), which monitors the quality of design throughout the United Kingdom.

Rahul Mehrotra is an Indian architect and urban designer trained at the School of Architecture, Ahmedabad, and the Graduate School of Design at Harvard University. He has been in private practice since 1990 and works on architecture, urban design and conservation projects. He has built extensively in India and, beside several single family houses, his projects include the Laxmi Machine Works Corporate Office in Coimbatore (1998), an Extension to the Prince of Wales Museum in Bombay (1995), the Institute for Rural Development in Tulzapur (2004), and the restoration of the Chowmahalla Palace in Hyderabad (phase 1 completed November 2004). He is currently developing (with the Taj Mahal Conservation Collaborative) a master plan for the conservation of the Taj Mahal and its surroundings. Professor Mehrotra is Executive Director of the Urban Design Research Institute, which promotes awareness and research on the city of Bombay. He has also written several books on Bombay, including *Bombay: the Cities Within* (2001), and has lectured extensively on urban design, conservation and architecture in India. His most recent book is *The Architecture of the 20th Century in the South Asian Region* (1999). He also serves on several government committees that are responsible for historic preservation and the conservation as well as creation of public spaces in Bombay. Rahul Mehrotra teaches at the University of Michigan, Ann Arbor, where he is an associate professor.

Farshid Moussavi is an architect of Iranian origin, trained at the Graduate School of Design at Harvard University, University College London, the Bartlett School of Architecture, London, and Dundee University. Before establishing Foreign Office Architects (FOA) with Alejandro Zaera Polo in London in 1992, she worked with the Renzo Piano Building Workshop in Genoa and the Office for Metropolitan Architecture in Rotterdam. Professor Moussavi taught at the Architectural Association in London from 1993 to 2000 and has been visiting professor at the University of California at Los Angeles, Columbia University in New York, Princeton University, the Berlage Institute in Amsterdam, and the Hoger Architecture Institute in Belgium. She is currently teaching at the Academy of Fine Arts in Vienna. FOA's built projects include a Passenger Cruise Terminal in Yokohama, Japan (2002) (awarded the RIBA Worldwide Award in 2004), a new park with outdoor auditoria in Barcelona (begun in 2004), the Bluemoon Hotel in Groningen, the Netherlands (2001), and a police headquarters in La Villajoyosa, Spain (2001). In the United Kingdom the practice is developing a master plan for the Lower Lee Valley in London, the 2012 London Olympics proposal, and a new Music Centre for the BBC, also in London. In 2002 FOA was one of the architectural practices shortlisted for the design of the new World Trade Center in New York. In the same year the practice represented Britain at the Eighth Venice Architecture Biennale, and a retrospective show of their work was mounted during 2003 at the Institute of Contemporary Arts, London.

Modjtaba Sadria is an Iranian-born philosopher and Professor at the Graduate School and Faculty of Policy Issues at Chuo University in Tokyo. Professor Sadria holds doctorate degrees in philosophy from the University of Paris and in international relations from the University of Quebec at Montreal, and master's degrees in literature, history and philosophy from the University of Paris. Professor Sadria is a specialist in cross-cultural relations and East Asian studies. He lectures widely, including recent presentations on 'A Complex World and Many Understandings' (Kobe, Japan, 2002), 'The Possibility of Dialogue After 9.11' (Tokyo, 2001), 'A Perspective of Iranian Foreign Policy: Triangle Relations between Khatami, Nation and Society' (Tokyo, 2000), 'Building Bridges between the United States and Iran' (Washington, D.C., 2002), and 'Preserving Cultural Integrity and Promoting Dialogue among Civilizations' (Tokyo, 1999). Professor Sadria is a member of the board of directors of the Institute of Policy and Culture, Tokyo, and from 1999 to 2001 he served as Deputy Director for Research at the International Center for Dialogue Among Civilizations in Tehran. Professor Sadria has published over fifty books and articles, including 'Social Development: Challenges to a Concept' (*Journal of Policy and Culture*, Tokyo, 2004) and 'East Asia: Cultural Aspects of Challenges in a Globalizing World' (*Globalization in East Asia*, 2004, in Japanese).

Reinhard Schulze is a German linguist and historian and professor of Islamic Studies at the University of Berne, Switzerland, where he is also Dean of the Faculty of Humanities. He studied Islam, Latin languages, Arabic and linguistics at the University of Bonn from 1974 to 1981, and went on to teach at the universities of Bochum, Bonn and Bamburg before joining the University of Berne in 1995. Professor Schulze is interested in the historical development and spread of Islam and in its contemporary under-standing and practice. His most important and recent work is *A Modern History of the Islamic World* (2000), and he has published social, economic and political studies of the Middle East, Asia and Africa, including 'The Birth of Tradition and Modernity in 18th and 19th Century Islamic Culture' (*History and Culture* 16, 1997), 'International Islamic Organizations and the Muslims in Europe' (*Migration* 28, 1998), 'Mass Culture and Islamic Culture Production in the 19th Century Middle East' (in *Mass Culture, Popular Culture, and Social Life in the Middle East*, edited by Georg Stauth and Sami Zubaida, 1987), 'The Forgotten Honor of Islam: The Muslim World in 1989' (in *Middle East Contemporary Survey XIII*, edited by Ami Ayalon, 1989), and 'Is there an Islamic Modernity?' (in *The Islamic World and the West*, edited by Kai Hafez, 1989).

Elías Torres Tur is a Spanish architect and partner in the firm Martínez Lapeña-Torres Arquitectos. Trained in architecture at the Escola Técnica Superior de Arquitectura de Barcelona (ETSAB), Mr Torres opened his private office with José Antonio Martínez Lapeña in Barcelona in 1968. Among their best-known projects are the Vila Olímpica Housing Complex in Barcelona (1994), the La Granja Escalator in Toledo (2001), the restoration of the Ronda Promenade in the City Walls at Palma de Mallorca (1990), the restoration of Antonio Gaudí's Park Güell in Barcelona (1993), and the Forum 2004 Esplanade and Photovoltaic Power Plant in Barcelona (1994), as well as several works in Japan including the Kumamoto Museum Annex (1994). The projects and completed works of Martínez Lapeña-Torres Arquitectos are widely exhibited and published in numerous monographs and catalogues and have received many architectural awards. Mr Torres has been a visiting professor at Harvard University and is currently a doctorate professor at ETSAB.

Billie Tsien is an American architect and artist trained in fine arts at Yale University and in architecture at the University of California at Los Angeles. She has worked with Tod Williams since 1977 and they have been in partnership since 1986. She has taught at the Parsons School of Design in New York, Yale University, Harvard University's Graduate School of Design, and the University of Texas at Austin. Completed works by Tod Williams Billie Tsien Architects include the American Museum of Folk Art in New York City (2001), the Student Arts Centre at Johns Hopkins University in Baltimore (2001), Feinberg Hall at Princeton University (1986), a 525-person dormitory and dining facility at the University of Virginia, Charlottesville (1994), a major addition to the Phoenix Art Museum (1996), the Natatorium at the Cranbrook School in Michigan (2000), and the Neurosciences Institute in La Jolla, California (1996). Ms Tsien has a particular interest in work that bridges art and architecture. She is an advisor for the Wexner Prize at Ohio State University, and serves on the boards of the Public Art Fund and the Architectural League, both in New York, and the American Academy of Rome. With Tod Williams, she is the recipient of the Brunner Award from the American Academy of Arts and Letters, the Medal of Honor from the New York City branch of the American Institute of Architects, the Thomas Jefferson Medal from the University of Virginia, and the Chrysler Award for Design Innovation. A monograph of their work entitled *Work Life* was published in 2000.

Jafar Tukan is a Jordanian architect trained at the American University of Beirut. After leaving university, he worked for the Jordanian Ministry of Public Works as a design architect and then joined the firm Dar Al-Handasah Consulting Engineers at their headquarter offices in Beirut. In 1968 he established a private practice in Beirut, and in 1973 formed the partnership Rais and Tukan Architects, which was later changed to Jafar Tukan and Partners Architects and Engineers and relocated to Amman. In 2003, he merged this firm with Consolidated Consultants for Engineering and the Environment. Mr Tukan's work has extended to nearly all aspects of architecture and planning and among his most notable projects are a new City Hall for Amman (1997), prototype kindergarten schools in Dubai (1980), the Jubilee High School in Amman (1999), and the SOS Children's Village in Aqaba, Jordan (1991), which was presented with an Aga Khan Award for Architecture in 2001. Mr Tukan is active in professional organizations for architecture, engineering, the protection of the historic built environment and fine arts in Jordan and Lebanon.

2004 Award Master Jury and Project Reviewers
Seated, left to right: Omar Abdulaziz Hallaj, Ghada Amer, Billie Tsien, Jimmy (Cheok Siang) Lim, Khadija Jamal-Shaban, Fernando Varanda, Hana Alamuddin, Shiraz Allibhai.
Standing, left to right: Yildirim Yavuz, Suha Özkan, Rahul Mehrotra, Sahel Al-Hiyari, Elias Torres Tur, Reinhard Schulze, Farshid Moussavi, Modjtaba Sadria, Jafar Tukan, Galal Abada, Hanif Kara, Mohammad Al-Asad, Farrokh Derakhshani. (Not pictured: Reha Günay, Michael Sorkin, Ayşil Yavuz.)

2004 Award Project Reviewers

Galal Abada is an Egyptian architect and urbanist and an assistant professor at Ain Shams University in Cairo, where he is also Director of the Historic Cairo Studies and Development Centre. Dr Abada studied at Ain Shams University, the School of Architecture Paris-Belleville, and the Catholic University of Leuven in Belgium. He has a PhD in architecture and urban design from Stuttgart University in Germany. His projects, including a number of winning competition entries, are located in Belgium, Germany and throughout the Middle East, particularly in Egypt. Current ongoing projects include a number of urban rehabilitation, adaptive reuse and design schemes in Egypt: a group of Children's Cultural Clubs in historic Cairo, the Cairo headquarters of the National Organization for Enhancing Urban Landscapes, the Museum of Qena, site planning and a visitors' centre for Dendara Temple and a proposed improvement project for the Luxor temples site. Dr Abada has been a member of the editorial board and a frequent contributor to the Egyptian architecture and design magazine *Medina*. During 2003, he was a member of the evalutation team for submissions to the international competition for the Great Egyptian Museum in Cairo.

Hana Alamuddin is a Lebanese architect who trained at Thames Polytechnic in the United Kingdom and at the Aga Khan Program for Islamic Architecture at Massachusetts Institute of Technology. She established her own architectural practice, Al-Mimariya, in Lebanon in 1998, and has completed many residential and restoration projects. She has been a lecturer at the American University of Beirut since 1994, where she teaches urban design and landscape architecture. Her recent teaching has concentrated on sustainable development with a focus on energy-efficient design in large-scale planning projects. Ms Alamuddin is a member of the executive committee of the Association pour la Protection des Sites et Anciennes Demeures au Liban (APSAD) and is actively involved in conservation projects in Lebanon, notably in Salimah. She served as a Project Reviewer during the 1998 and 2001 cycles of the Award.

Mohammad Al-Asad is a Jordanian architect and architectural historian and the founding director of the Center for the Study of the Built Environment in Amman. He studied architecture at the University of Illinois at Urbana-Champaign and history of architecture at Harvard University, before taking post-doctoral research positions at Harvard and at the Institute for Advanced Study, Princeton. He has taught at the University of Jordan, Princeton University, Massachusetts Institute of Technology and the University of Illinois at Urbana-Champaign, where he was the Alan K. and Leonarda Laing Distinguished Visiting Professor. Dr al-Asad has published in both Arabic and English on the architecture of the Islamic world in books and academic and professional journals. He is the author of *Old Houses of Jordan: Amman 1920–1950* (1997), and co-author (with Ghazi Bisheh and Fawzi Zayadine) of *The Umayyads: The Rise of Islamic Art* (2000). Dr Al-Asad is a member of the board of directors of the Jordan National Gallery of Fine Arts, a part of the Royal Society for Fine Arts. He served as a Project Reviewer for the Aga Khan Award for Architecture during the 1989, 1995 and 1998 Award cycles.

Sahel Al-Hiyari is a Jordanian architect and painter. He studied architecture and fine arts at the Rhode Island School of Design, and received a master's degree in urban design from Harvard University. He later undertook doctoral studies in architecture at the University of Venice. He has worked at Dar Al-Handasah (Shair and Partners) in Cairo and Machado Silvetti Associates in Boston, and is now the principal in the architectural firm Sahel Al-Hiyari and Partners. In 2003, Mr Al-Hiyari was the first architect honoured by the Rolex Mentor and Protégé Arts Initiative and has since worked closely with the architect Alvaro Siza in Portugal. Mr Al-Hiyari's paintings have been exhibited in Jordan, Lebanon and Italy.

Reha Günay is a Turkish architect, restoration architect and architectural photographer, and Professor of Conservation and Restoration at Yildiz Technical University Faculty of Architecture, Istanbul. Professor Günay also teaches architectural photography at Mimar Sinan University in Istanbul. He was trained in architecture at Istanbul Technical University, and received his PhD from Istanbul University in the Faculty of Arts and Letters, joining the Faculty of Architecture in 1973. During 1979–80 Professor Günay was a fellow of the Japan Foundation. He has been working on the restoration of the antique theatre in Side, Turkey, since 1992. Professor Günay's research, essays and photography have been published as monographs, including *Japanese Art and Culture Through the Ages* (1986), *Places and Expression: Techniques in the Miniatures of the Süleymanname* (1992), *Tradition of the Turkish House and Safranbolu Houses* (1998), *Sinan: the Architect and His Works* (1998) and *Traditional Wooden Buildings: Problems and Solutions* (2002). He has also published on the topic of architectural restoration and conservation, and contributed photographs to numerous art historical publications and monographs on leading architects in Turkey. Professor Günay has contributed research and photography to the Aga Khan Award for Architecture since 1983.

Omar Abdulaziz Hallaj is a Syrian architect in private practice in Aleppo and a partner in the Suradec Consortium (Sustainable Urban Rehabilitation, Architectural Design and Engineering). Mr Hallaj had served in the past as the Chairman of the Technical Committee responsible for the preservation of the old city of Aleppo, supervising implementation of rehabilitation measures and coordinating integrated interventions for the preservation of historic neighbourhoods in Aleppo. He has most recently been involved in the development of the Historic Houses Programme of the Shibam Urban Development Project in Yemen. Mr Hallaj was trained at the University of Texas at Austin, where he received both his bachelor's and master's degrees in architecture. He continues to research the development of architecture and urban theory in the context of historic and contemporary Muslim societies, and is particularly interested and active in community-oriented planning and urban management. Mr Hallaj served as a Project Reviewer during the 1998 and 2001 Award cycles.

Khadija Jamal-Shaban is a Pakistani architect and planner who studied at the Aga Khan Program for Islamic Architecture at Massachusetts Institute of Technology and the NED University of Engineering and Technology in Karachi. Ms Jamal-Shaban works in the fields of design, planning and development and is committed to improving the quality of human life through the built environment. Her work has been located in Afghanistan, Tajikistan, the Kyrgyz Republic and Kazakhstan, as well as in Pakistan, and she has been a consultant to such agencies as the World Bank, the Swiss Development Cooperation, the US Agency for International Development, the Aga Khan Development Network and other non-governmental organizations. Ms Jamal-Shaban is a visiting faculty member of the NED University of Engineering and Technology, where she advises final-year thesis students. She is an active member of the Institute of Architects of Pakistan, working to improve professional standards in the country. Ms Jamal-Shaban served as a Project Reviewer during the 2001 Award cycle.

Jimmy (Cheok Siang) Lim is a Malaysian architect, trained at the University of New South Wales in Sydney. From 1972 to 1977 he was senior architect and then an associate of Project Architects Sdn in Kuala Lumpur, and he established his own practice, CSL Associates, in 1978. His built works, both in Malaysia and abroad, have ranged from residential bungalows to high- and low-rise commercial complexes, medical facilities, sporting facilities and hotels and resorts. He is the architect of the Salinger Residence in Selangor, Malaysia, which received an Aga Khan Award for Architecture during the 1998 Award cycle. In 1983, Mr Lim was a founding member and trustee of the Heritage Trust of Malaysia (Badan Warisan Malaysia), and he continues to serve as a member of the Trust Council. He served as President of the Friends of Heritage of Malaysia (Sahabat Warisan Malaysia) from 1998 to 1992, and was President of the Malaysian Architectural Institute from 1991 to 1993. Mr Lim is active in local residents' organizations in Kuala Lumpur, working to resist uncontrolled planning, prevent destruction of the environment and protect the natural environment and ecology of the city. He has presented numerous papers on architecture and conservation at seminars and conferences in Malaysia and internationally.

Michael Sorkin is the principal of the Michael Sorkin Studio in New York City, a design practice devoted to both practical and theoretical projects at all scales, with a special interest in the city. Recent projects include master planning in Hamburg (1998) and Schwerin (1999), Germany; planning for a Palestinian capital in East Jerusalem (1999); urban design in Leeds, United Kingdom (2003); campus planning at the University of Chicago (1998); and City College of New York studies of the Manhattan waterfront, Far Rockaway (1994), and a large park in Queens Plaza (1997). The studio is the recipient of a variety of awards, including three *ID* Awards and a *Progressive Architecture* Award. Professor Sorkin is the Director of the Graduate Urban Design Program at the City College of New York. From 1993 to 2000 he was Professor of Urbanism and Director of the Institute of Urbanism at the Academy of Fine Arts in Vienna. Previously, he has been professor at numerous schools of architecture including the Cooper Union, New York (for ten years) and the universities of Columbia, Yale (holding both Davenport and Bishop chairs), Harvard, Cornell (Gensler Chair), Nebraska (Hyde Chair), Illinois, Pennsylvania, Texas and Minnesota. Professor Sorkin lectures widely and is the author of many articles in a wide range of both professional and general publications and is currently contributing editor at *Architectural Record* and *Metropolis*. For ten years, he was the architecture critic of *The Village Voice*. His books include *Variations on A Theme Park* (1991), *Exquisite Corpse* (1991), *Wiggle* (a monograph of his studio's work, 1998), *The Next Jerusalem* (2002), *Starting From Zero* (2003), and *Analyzing Ambasz* (2004). Forthcoming in 2005 are *Fifteen Minutes in Manhattan, Against The Wall* and *Work on the City*. Michael Sorkin was born in Washington, D.C., and received his architectural training at Harvard University and Massachusetts Institute of Technology.

Fernando Varanda is a Portuguese architect and urban planner. He graduated in architecture from the Lisbon School of Fine Arts, received his master's degree in urban and regional planning from New York University and was awarded a PhD in human geography from Durham University in the United Kingdom. He is currently a professor in the department of urbanism at the Universidade Lusófona in Lisbon. Since 1973, he has undertaken extensive research on built spaces in Yemen, published in both monographs and specialized publications, notably *The Art of Building in Yemen* (1982). He has also undertaken research into the built environments of Portugal, and published *Mértola no Alengarve* in 2002. Dr Varanda is in private practice in Lisbon, woking on a variety of projects for the public and private sectors, especially those involving the rehabilitation of buildings and building technologies, as well as the integration of new structures in historic centres. Dr Varanda served as a Project Reviewer during the 1986, 1998 and 2001 cycles of the Award.

Ayşıl Yavuz is a Turkish restoration architect with doctorate degrees in conservation from the University of Rome and from Istanbul Technical University. She has been a staff member of the Department of Restoration at Middle East Technical University in Ankara since its foundation, and she also teaches restoration design and historic structural systems there, and serves as a thesis director for master's and doctoral students. Professor Yavuz was the Chair of the Department of Interior Architecture at King Faisal University, Damman, Saudi Arabia, from 1982 to 1988. She has taken part in and directed several pilot conservation and restoration projects in Turkey, and is widely published in English and Turkish on the topics of conservation, structure and construction and the architecture of caravanserais. Her most recent fieldwork has taken place in Turkmenistan for the restoration of the Sultan Sanjar Mausoleum in Merv, and in Turkey for the restoration of Alara Han, a Seljuk caravanserai in Antalya, and the restoration of the museum–mansion of Atatürk at Cankaya in Ankara. Professor Yavuz served as a Project Reviewer for the 1998 and 2001 Award cycles.

Yıldırım Yavuz is a Turkish architect, faculty member and former dean of the Middle East Technical University (METU) School of Architecture in Ankara. Professor Yavuz received bachelor's and master's degrees in architecture from METU, and a second master's degree in architecture from the University of Pennsylvania. He taught architectural design and history at METU from 1962 to 1982 and design and history of architecture at King Faisal University, Damman, Saudi Arabia, from 1982 to 1988. He then became Vice-Dean of the Faculty of Art, Design and Architecture at Bilkent University, Ankara, where he taught advanced design at graduate level and art and culture at undergraduate level. Professor Yavuz has served as a member of many national committees for cultural affairs and architecture in Turkey and his research is concentrated on architectural history of the nineteenth and twentieth centuries. He is also active as an architect and is currently designing a Nationality Classroom at the University of Pittsburgh in the United States. He served as a Project Reviewer during the 1992, 1995 and 2001 Award Cycles.

The Award Secretariat

Suha Özkan, Secretary General, has been associated with the Aga Khan Award for Architecture since 1982. Having studied architecture at the Middle East Technical University (METU) in Ankara, he went to the Architectural Association in London to study theory of design. He taught architectural design and design theory at METU for fifteen years, becoming Associate Dean of the Faculty of Architecture in 1978 and Vice-President of the university in 1979. On behalf of the Aga Khan Trust for Culture he has organized three international architectural competitions – for the Revitalization of Samarkand, Uzbekistan (1991), the new Museum of Islamic Arts in Doha, Qatar (1997), and the Doha Corniche and Arts and Culture Plaza (2003). In 2002, Dr Özkan was elected as a Council Member (Region II) of the International Union of Architects (UIA), and will be President of the UIA's twenty-second Congress to be held in Istanbul during 2005. He was made an honorary fellow of the American Institute of Architects in 2004.

Farrokh Derakhshani Director of Award Procedures
Siméon Duchoud Documentalist
Jack Kennedy Executive Officer
William O'Reilly Librarian, Aga Khan Trust for Culture
Mariam Panosetti Award Procedures Assistant
Karen Stylianoudis Executive Secretary

Photo Credits
Galal Abada: 125; Kamran Adle: 124, 125, 130–7;
Hana Alamuddin: 18, 19; Rémy Audouin: 70, 80;
Marylène Barret: 70, 71, 76, 77, 82; Cal Earth: 54, 55,
57, 58–9, 60–1, 62–3; Pierre-Yves Dhinaut: 138–9,
170–3; Siméon Duchoud: 36, 37, 40–9; Cemal
Emden: 106, 107, 109–19; Diébédo Francis Kéré: 36,
37; Murat German: 71, 74–5, 78–9, 81, 88, 89, 92–3,
Reha Günay: 70, 71; Dada Krpasundarananda: 54,
Mohamed Nafea: 18, 30–1; OCJRP: 88; Christian
Richters: 18, 19, 22–9; Steve Sabella: 88, 89, 94–101;
Modjtaba Sadria: 149; Fujita Tadayoshi: 149;
UNDP Tehran: 55, 64–5; Ayşıl Yavuz: 70.
Pages 157–67
Abdelhalim I. Abdelhalim, Abdel Wahid El-Wakil,
Kamran Adle, Mohammad Akram, Hana
Alamuddin, Mokhless Al-Hariri, Yori Antar,
Arriyadh Development Authority, Chant
Avedissian, Jacques Bétant, Timothy Bradley,
Steven Cohn, Argun Dundar, Abdel Wahed El-
Wakil, Cemal Emden, Monica Fritz, Seiichi Furuya,
Reha Günay, Güven Incirlioglu, Barry Iverson,
Sian Kennedy, Saleh Lamei-Mostafa, Christian
Lignon, Christopher Little, Pascal Maréchaux,
Khedija M'Hadhebi, Kamel Nefzi, K. L. Ng, John
Paniker, Jacques Perez, Ram Rahman, Christian
Richters, Samir Saddi, Hans Scholten, Skidmore,
Owings & Merrill and Rajesh Vora.

Drawings
All drawings were provided by the architects.

Documentation assistance
at the Award Secretariat in Geneva was provided
by: Thê-Hông Tang-Lâm (team leader), Minh
Phung Dào, Hoàng Long Dô, Truòng Vy Duong,
Vuong Son Duong, Dình Khoa Kristian Hoàng,
Thuy An Hoàng, Duy Nhiên Lâm-Bình, Bao Trân
Lâm, Karine Kim Lan Lê-Van, Ngoc Phu Mai,
Quôc An Nguyên, Tiên Dung Nguyên, Thi Lê Thu
Nguyên-Ngoc, Kim Phuong Pham, Ngoc Hô Pham
and Nhu Huy Trân. Special thanks to Pamela
Johnston, Laura Hobson and Shiraz Allibhai.

The Aga Khan Award for Architecture
P.O. Box 2049
1211 Geneva 2
Switzerland
www.akdn.org